CHOOSE
YOUR
PERSPECTIVE

BOOKS BY JOHN MARTIN

Empower Yourself

Increase Your Personal Productivity

Choose Your Perspective

CHOOSE
YOUR
PERSPECTIVE

7 TIPS FOR
HIGH PERFORMANCE
THROUGH
INTENTIONAL THINKING

JOHN MARTIN

Published and Distributed by
SOUND WISDOM
PO Box 310
Shippensburg, PA 17257-0310
717-530-2122
info@soundwisdom.com
www.soundwisdom.com

While efforts have been made to verify information contained in this publication, neither the author nor the publisher assumes any responsibility for errors, inaccuracies, or omissions. While this publication is chock-full of useful, practical information, it is not intended to be legal or accounting advice. All readers are advised to seek competent lawyers and accountants to follow laws and regulations that may apply to specific situations. The reader of this publication assumes responsibility for the use of the information. The author and publisher assume no responsibility or liability whatsoever on the behalf of the reader of this publication.

Cover/Jacket designer Eileen Rockwell
Interior designed by Susan Ramundo

ISBN 13 TP: 978-1-64095-142-6
ISBN 13 eBook: 978-1-64095-143-3

For Worldwide Distribution, Printed in the U.S.A.
1 2 3 4 5 6 / 22 21 20 19

When you change the way you look at things,
the things you look at change.—Max Planck

CONTENTS

Introduction   11

1   Awareness   17

2   Acceptance and Action   43

3   Positivity   67

4   Productivity   83

5   Patience   99

6   Creativity   125

7   Empathy and Gratitude   143

Conclusion   165

About the Author   175

INTRODUCTION

What is your perspective?

The way you see things is one way to put it. The feeling of "I am" or "I think" is another style of describing this idea of perspective. It's the way we think, the way we see life, right?

But wait—there's more! There is a way of controlling this outlook—a way of *not* accepting perspective at face value, but instead *choosing* your perspective and using this outlook to your advantage.

You don't always choose your thoughts—but you can choose which thoughts you contemplate further and you can choose which thoughts to discard or push from your mind immediately. You can choose which thoughts you act upon. This is the foundation of choosing your perspective, your view of life. When you fully grasp the potential of this ability, you can improve your entire mindset and your experiences in life.

Being able to change your perspective regardless of your situation is critical to achieving your goals and enjoying everyday life, because controlling your perspective means you can control your feelings and emotions to a large extent. Your emotions are often what dictate your actions without the least bit of intentional mental awareness on your part.

Our emotions often dictate actions without any intentional mental awareness on our part.

Controlling and choosing your perspective doesn't come quickly and even the actual shift in perspective itself doesn't always happen instantly—although it may. Sometimes you have to sit with a situation and turn it around in your mind to see it from different angles, like turning a puzzle piece to see which way it fits into the puzzle as a whole.

So how do you change the way you look at a thing? How do you change your perspective of a negative situation? Or how do you change your view of the monotonous to make it more meaningful and inspiring?

In the following chapters, I offer tools that will help you transform your perspective through intentional thinking.

When you master your mind, you will bring powerful improvement to your daily life, and it all begins with becoming aware of your thoughts.

Recognizing thoughts from an outside view, as the watcher of thoughts rather than the thinker, establishes the building blocks for intentional thinking. Through this mild detachment, you can see ideologies, definitions, or labels that you always held as true are actually stories or beliefs formed by repeated thoughts that you either accepted without questioning (observation) or that originated in another person's mind and were passed on to you, often during childhood. Once you are able to distance the idea of self from thoughts, you are on the first step toward freedom through the ability to choose your own perspective.

As you examine thoughts and beliefs, you will keep some and you will discard others. You may even find yourself living in a situation that is incompatible with the views or beliefs you now hold and the ones you've thrown away. You will experience an increase of what psychologists call cognitive dissonance and you will feel like you are in an uncomfortable wrestling match with your thoughts. A common question at this stage is, "How do I know when to change my perspective of my circum-stances and when to change my circumstances?" It's true that sometimes no matter how you turn the puzzle piece, it doesn't fit into the part of the puzzle you are working on. So you will need to decide what to accept and what to take action on.

This is the next tool for developing intentional thinking. It will be important to learn how to be productive in negative circumstances in order to follow through with the action that will lead to your eventual change in circumstances. There are many ways to influence this productivity including healthy ways to alter your mind and body for maximum success.

And remember, patience is essential even if you feel it is not in your genetic makeup to be patient. It may seem as if there is not enough time and you are too far behind schedule to be patient. You may feel as if you have not done enough or you are not reaching your goals quickly enough. But there are new and different ways to think about time that can benefit you immediately *and* in the long run. There are tools that can be used habitually to discover time and use patience in the most hectic of schedules.

The fun part comes into play once you have learned how to use patience, discernment, and awareness of thought to calm your mind and control your perspective—now you can be creative.

All around you and into your mind, new ideas and thoughts will arise that were previously buried by all the stress and endless mental chatter, stories of the remembered past and imagined future. With the ability to discard those stories as you see fit, not only will you be more creative, you will also have the ability to concentrate and follow through on bringing those inspired ideas to fruition. Many of these seemingly original ideas will be observed in the most familiar of circumstances. You might even

Intentional thinking is a lifelong process.

experience that proverbial sensation of realizing that what you had been spending your life looking for was right in front of you all along!

Try it out. Choose your perspective. Use these tools in your daily life and share your results with others. Sharing your story is a way of spreading the wealth and generosity of ideas. We live in one of the most opportunity-laden eras in history, and the Internet has given us so many more ways to offer and consume information, to help each other and to spread positivity.

When you are feeling low, think about something to be thankful for—there is so much good to see. That attitude of gratitude will force you to be optimistic about life and soon the bad feelings will be replaced with an uplifted spirit and hope for the hour, the day, and the week. Spread positivity whenever you feel it—trust me, someone needs it. Even if others give you a hard time because they want to remain in their own self-pity or sadness, keep spreading your positive outlook to whomever you encounter. Someone(s) will be glad you do!

Intentional thinking is a lifelong process and goal, and there will be days when you fail to maintain your chosen outlook—maybe you lose your temper, identify with your stress, get depressed, and make a poor decision as a result. When you fail, it is important to once again use your tools to choose your perspective and try again.

Try again.

You have everything to gain and nothing to lose.

CHAPTER ONE

AWARENESS

*Consciousness is the perception of what
passes in a man's own mind.*—John Locke

What are you thinking?

What if you could even momentarily—just long enough
for a look—see from a perspective outside of your reality,
outside of your mind?

If possible, take some time right now and go look into a
mirror. Look at the reflection of your face and body and
try to disassociate from the reflection. You are seeing only
a reflection; it's not you. Let this sink in, slowly—give it
time, and then try to imagine that you have no name.
Peel away layer after layer of your identity—mother,
father, daughter, little sister, older or younger brother,
spouse or ex, employee, employer, entrepreneur, business owner, project manager, accountant, retail associate,

construction worker, etc. Now what do you see? Take a moment and realize how much of your reality and identity is made up of thoughts, names, and labels—nothing but words and ideas.

Continuing to look in the mirror, observe and recognize your breathing and the continuous thoughts passing through your mind. Notice the random nature of your thinking. Maybe you are noticing your eyebrows need plucked or shaped, or maybe you need to shave. Maybe your hair needs a trim, it's graying or getting thinner, or you think you could lose some weight. All of a sudden, you think about an email from work or an item you need to pick up at the store. What should I have for dinner tonight? Then you think of a friend or your child…and on and on.

Notice how random and uncontrolled your thoughts are and yet how much weight you give them when constructing your reality.

CENTER OF THE UNIVERSE

We live our lives as if we are at the center of all reality, and of course, that is what it feels like. Everything is happening to us. Or so it seems.

You know intellectually that you are not in the center of reality, that in fact you are but one of billions of other human beings, let alone other species of life, on a huge planet amid innumerable other planets in the universe.

What does all this have to do with being aware of thoughts? Well, it takes practice, but if you can let go and separate from that feeling of "I am," your ego, you can see that thoughts arise from outside of what you consider "you" and that means you can watch them appear in your mind, you can watch them leave, you can choose to focus on which ones to keep and continue thinking about.

THOUGHTS AND EMOTIONS

Unobserved, thoughts drift into your mind without prompting. They seem to float up and around and they go deeper into a direction pulling out new details—more thoughts—triggering and then exacerbating an emotional response that flows through the body as a result of the thought. More thoughts come from the added emotion. The emotion grows stronger and initiates more thoughts by virtue of the nervous system's reaction to and symptoms of the emotion itself.

Your actions are influenced by chain thinking.

Then our actions are influenced by this chain of thinking. What we do depends on that line of thoughts that we followed and then our actions, of course, continue the train of thought and initiate new thoughts as well—*a loop system of action feeding thoughts and thoughts feeding action.* Are you trapped in this system? It may feel like you are.

CONNECTED BUT DIFFERENT

The mind is controllable to a greater extent than is some-times realized. If you start getting outside of it just for a couple seconds of time, you can see the world—your world—as just that. Your world. It's your story. Your perspective on life is a story that is unfolding on the video camera of your mind; and while you are connected to all of life as a phenomenon, your experience is different from every other person's experience.

Even the similarities to other humans such as attending the same school, being born of the same mother, working at the same company, doing the same job, living in the same house and so on—all these experiences that you might share with another individual take place in different minds and therefore, the focus is on different details, different words, images, and emotions in each experience. Paradoxical, but it makes sense when you think about how you perceive the world around you as you move through it.

Imagine your eyes or ears, any of your sensory abilities as a recorder of an experience.

PERCEPTIONS OF REALITY

Have you ever wondered about other's perceptions of you as you move through their camera's lenses? Or about how you see life happen every day, moving around you? When traveling in your vehicle, do you notice the speed at which the buildings, signs, other vehicles, and people pass by you? Or you pass by them?

The images, the sounds, the activities, the buzz of life are all inside your mind, do you see? There's no sound without a mind to perceive it. This shouldn't sound like fluffy high-minded nonsense, because it's not, it's close to earth, here beside you. These observations are what can allow a person to stay cool and calm in a nerve-wracking situation. If it's true that our life is largely impacted by our perception, then it follows that we should have some control over that perception. Our actions should impact our perception.

PERCEPTION VERSUS PERSPECTIVE

Perspective is the way you see life while *perception* is the way you understand what you see. Think of perspective as the filter or the coloring of your lenses—for example rose-colored glasses—and perception as your operating system, the way things look after you download them through your filtered mind. How do you interpret the images you see?

Perspective and perception work together and they work separately. And though they are similar, they are useful in different ways when it comes to gaining the benefits of controlling and harnessing the power of perspective. The way you perceive life is less controllable than the way you see life. Meaning, it's easier to put an optimistic spin on what you see than it is to maintain that optimistic feeling after the images have come and gone and you are left with your mind alone and how it decodes the information it has received.

As "New Thought Pioneer" Prentice Mulford pointed out, "Every thought of yours is a real thing—a force." He also said:

> When you say to yourself, "I am going to have a pleasant visit or a pleasant journey," you are literally sending elements and forces ahead of your body that will arrange things to make your visit or journey pleasant. When before the visit or the journey or the shopping trip you are in a bad humour, or fearful or apprehensive of something unpleasant, you are sending unseen agencies ahead of you which will make some kind of unpleasantness. Our thoughts, or in other words, our state of mind, is ever at work "fixing up" things good or bad in advance.

You know that things start from thoughts, but how do you channel and control your thoughts and the way you perceive daily life?

Consider for a moment how two people see something different when looking at the same thing. Take, for example, the commonly seen pictures where some people will immediately see one image, while others see a different image. How can this be?

We are all living in our own worlds made of mental constructions that differ from person to person and so it is important not to expect others to see things the way we do—even if we may want them to. It is the variety of views that makes life interesting, a mixed bag of perspectives makes for fascinating culture. This is a basic foundation piece of understanding and harnessing the power of perspective.

Scientist and writer Isaac Asimov said, "Show me someone who can't understand people and I'll show you someone who has built up a false image of himself."

It's important to understand that people will see things differently and the way you see yourself is not necessarily the way others see you.

A mixed bag of perspectives makes for fascinating culture.

LEARNING FROM EACH OTHER

Considering each person's unique perspective of life, every very person has something more to learn, as well as having something to teach, or share. When we talk about judgment and self-judgment, we are essentially talking about external and internal perspectives. For example, someone criticizes us and we take that criticism personally and feel hurt or ashamed—we have self-judged by believing what the other person said. It's our perspective of self, our internal perspective.

If you walk down the street and see someone carefully groomed, dressed in an expensive suit, and getting into the back of a limousine, you may judge that person as rich and successful. When you walk by and say hi, and the person doesn't return the greeting, maybe you judge him or her as a snob. It may turn out that the person didn't hear you. It may also turn out that the clothing and pretentious ride is a ruse.

Preconceived perspectives and judgments are often wrong.

Our judgments are often wrong. Whether about ourselves or others, superficial judgments can get in the way of learning. If you think someone who is homeless can't teach you anything about life, you may rob yourself of much knowledge. One of the most interesting conversations I've ever had about religion was with a man who was homeless, a "traveler," he called himself, bearded and dirty. He commented on a couple of titles I was holding while sitting in the library. We ended up talking for a long time about different religious ideas and history and books and life in general. And he had read everything I could imagine and then some.

Based on my superficial judgments of his appearance, I would have never predicted this man's mental lucidity and well-read background.

Try not to dismiss someone's ideas or thoughts because you consider the person unintelligent. Intelligence can be measured many different ways; realize that each person you interact with is more intelligent than you in some area. See what you can learn instead of indulging the ego's false sense of intelligence.

YOU *WILL* GET IT DONE

It is easy to get overwhelmed with to-do lists, with emails that need responses, and with phone calls that require responses. In order to get a proper perspective on daily work, chores, errands, etc., begin with the belief that you will accomplish every task. You will finish all the things on your list and you will manage to juggle everything else that life throws your way in the meantime. It is crucial to start from this place of thinking—this perspective.

Of course that does not take away the stress of the moment. For example, when things continue to pile on top of your already full plate, it is hard to take a moment and breathe. That is the secret. Step back from your desk, work station, or your planner and breathe—several deep breaths bring calmness to chaos.

Understand that the stress is imagined, the worry of not getting things done, is imagined. You will get done what needs to be done. When you worry, it is just your ego playing tricks on you. It is the ego asserting its importance as your sole identity and personality and claiming its spot in front of what you could and should be focusing your attention on.

When you worry, your ego is playing tricks on you.

Your ego wants you to doubt yourself and procrastinate from doing what you could be doing to actually help with those overwhelming feelings. If you are steadily chipping away at your list, you are not spending time worrying and imagining worst case scenarios and feeding the pain of self-importance that your ego thrives on. The illusory idea that you are your personality and your ego can cause you to withdraw deeper into your thoughts and worries and never get anything accomplished.

IT'S A MIRACLE TO BE ALIVE!

Let go of the pressure to perform. Of course there is the need to play a role in many circumstances in life, but remember that it is only a role. It is not who you are. Find peace during pressure in knowing that it is all part of a miraculous experience we call being alive.

Many times as a goal-oriented individual, the pressure to succeed can weigh you down and actually inhibit your ability to work effectively toward your aspirations. The effect of being super goal-oriented can have a counter-intuitive effect on your life in general. You want success, and anything short of your imagined version is thought to be a failure.

How do you change your outlook in regard to your ideals of succeeding in life? First, take the pressure of time and remove it from your thoughts whenever possible. Exercise patience as frequently as possible—make it second nature. Patience in all situations can help defuse stress and anger as well as allow you to make better decisions.

Second, try not to judge yourself as successful or unsuccessful based on specific goals and achievements or lack thereof. Your life is made up of many, many endeavors, and when you see your work as an entirety, you can be more

Release self-induced stress to control your perspective.

appreciative of your efforts and accomplishments. Less self-judgement and less hurry, coincidentally, allow you to end up building and achieving more in a shorter amount of time.

When you release self-induced stress, you are one step closer to controlling your perspective. Kill the demons by not feeding them with internal pressure, resistance, and self-doubt. Find passion in doing.

READ MORE BOOKS

Reading is one of the best ways to alter your consciousness, widen your perspective, and gain the benefit of learning from the perspectives of many others. Fiction, nonfiction, graphic novels, trade magazines—they are all helpful in learning more about the experiences of life and the world you live in. Culturally, geographically, scientifically, spiritually, and in many other ways books can be instructive as well as interesting and fun.

Reading a book has the power to change your belief system for the better. Reading has the power to change the way you live and the way you see life. This is no small thing. The written word is so powerful that advertising agencies spend millions and millions of dollars each year on getting the ad copy just right. The words you see on billboards, in magazine ads, and television commercials have tons of money and thought behind them because of the power of words to inspire millions of dollars in consumerism.

The more you read, the better you can communicate using the written word. Reading means you are sharing the mind of another. You are connecting to another person's consciousness through reading the words the writer has written.

The more you read, the better you can communicate.

The beneficial usefulness of reading is multiplied with each book you read. So if you read four books, you have gained access to the perspective of four other people—their thoughts, their beliefs, their worldview and perspective. You then have the choice to absorb those different points of view for your betterment or to discard what isn't to your benefit.

In addition, reading books is a perfect way to escape your own reality and your own perspective for a while, although you will still be reading the author's writings with your filter of life experience and life goals coloring and interpreting the words. Reading gives us a way of communicating with those who have passed before us—those who are gone but whose words live forever and touch people's hearts and mind hundreds and even thousands of years later.

When you use a book to, say, fix a car engine, it changes your perspective, increases your knowledge. Maybe you use a how-to book to fix a computer problem or find a new recipe. Whatever the case, perhaps the task before you is intimidating, something you've never done before; and frankly, you're not sure if you can do it. Yet you follow the steps outlined in the book and stick with the process and eventually you succeed in completing the activity.

You were successful by reading accumulated and shared knowledge in the book. Now that you have the knowledge in your own mind, you no longer believe that the task is overwhelming or impossible for you to complete. This adds a layer to your confidence and your abilities in life. Anything that reduces self-doubt or overthinking is a tool for choosing your perspective.

Another interesting method of intentional thinking comes when you consider the idea of acting spontaneously.

SPONTANEITY

When you act in a spontaneous manner, it doesn't mean necessarily that you are acting quickly or hastily. It sometimes means doing the thing that is most truthful of you. The truest action you can take is *sometimes* the first action or thought that comes to mind. I emphasize the word "sometimes." In some instances, the first thing that comes to mind may be the very worst choice you could make. Choosing your perspective includes learning how to notice and then differentiate those variances.

Consider: When are you acting impulsively and when are you acting authentically? Is your impulsive act also an authentic one? When should you rethink the act you are drawn to and when should you not think about it at all?

The goal is to embrace a perspective that allows for more authentic, courageous actions for the activities that you want to do. Sometimes the work that comes naturally to you is overthought and dismissed due to second guessing. It's not just in work that this is important to consider. It is also true in relationships, parenting, and even hobbies.

Embrace an authentically you perspective.

Don't allow yourself and your ego to talk you out of behaving from a perspective that is uniquely your own and that will allow you to have an even broader, more inclusive and insightful perspective on the world and your place in it. This is your choice—to see the world as negative or positive.

CHOOSE YOUR WORLD

Albert Einstein said, "I'd rather be an optimist and a fool than a pessimist and right." Whatever you choose as your overriding view and vibe of the world is what you get back. If you see the world as an evil or as a curse, you will see and attract evidence to support that view. And of course, the reverse is true. If you see the world and people as good and friendly, you will notice and draw pleasant energy into your life to support that worldview.

This perspective is important to understand even if you come from horrible circumstances. If you have been through tragedy after tragedy, still this is relevant and true because you are here now and you have opportunities to change your current perspective. It is true that there are evil, sadness, and heartache as part of life, but it is no less true that there are genuine joy, goodness, and people who are willing to help you. What will you focus on—the beauty or ugliness of life?

What you focus on is magnified. Like a microscope, when you point your mind—view and thoughts—toward an idea or object, it becomes bigger and more important in your perspective. The aspects of it become

With a positive perspective on life, you see beauty, good, and usefulness in everything!

clearer to you than if it remained in your peripheral or in the background, nearly ignored. Now if you have a negative filter over your glasses or if you favor a pessimistic perspective, you will see all these newly shown parts of the idea or the object as bad or harmful or whatever piece of negativity they might possess. But if you have a positive perspective on life, you will find the beauty, the good, and the usefulness of the thing, no matter what.

WHAT YOU KNOW WILL SHOW

Your perspective on your abilities, on your path, and general view of life will manifest itself in your life in a million different ways. What do you know? Do you know what you are good at? Do you know what fulfills you on a daily basis? What about a lifetime—are you content with and thankful for the life you've lived if today was your last day?

Know that everything will be alright, everything will always work out alright. Stick with what you know. Let your knowledge guide you rather than your worries or fears. Instead of wondering what the ever-changing world of technology might do to your business or your hobby, keep doing what you know you do well.

Stay strong in what you know and be true to yourself.

Adaptation will come about naturally if you let it. Relying on what you know is the first step to letting in the new knowledge that may be necessary to succeed in your field. Stay strong in what you know and what you've experienced to be true about yourself and your life. That confidence will take you through the hard times.

SELF-CONFIDENCE

One of the secret ingredients to harnessing the power of perspective is confidence. Confidence itself is an idea with many variations or expressions and interpretations. It is helpful to have your own definition of words that are used frequently like this one. For me, confidence means believing I can do what I think I can do.

In your mind, words can take on imagery that is far more grandiose than they need to be. This in turn can help to convince you that you are not confident because your personality does not match that of the person you imagine to be representative of confidence. But there are many forms of confidence. Define and embrace your own form of confidence, and you will find a changed perspective that will empower you to do many things that you wished to do, but had escaped you due to wrong beliefs about your personality.

For example, you may think you could climb Mount Everest, but if it came down to having the opportunity to do it or wanting to do it, you might talk yourself out of it because of limited belief. Belief in your ability is the next step after knowing you can do something. Belief leads to action and allows you to follow through and complete your goals.

> *Belief in your ability is the next step after knowing you can do something.*

PARANOIA

For the purpose of this writing, let's accept the meaning of paranoid to be fearful or suspicious of ill-will, wrong doing, or impending negative circumstances without evidence to justify that suspicion. Paranoia is a little different from pessimism in that it is usually relegated to a specific time in one's life that is set in motion by something that is said or something that happens outside of one's control. Pessimism is more constant.

Paranoia paralyzes the mind in a way. It affects the perspective so deeply that only an outsider can really recognize and point it out once a person is in the grips of it. Listen to a trusted friend or acquaintance if they tell you that you are being paranoid. There's a chance they are telling the truth and you are so caught up in your winding thoughts that snowball into negativity that you don't notice or realize the source of them. It's worrying about what hasn't happened.

Paranoia paralyzes your mind.

DON'T TRUST THOUGHTS

Pay attention to the ease with which your mind and mood can change. To do this, I recommend recording and transcribing as many thoughts as possible throughout an entire day or two or longer if possible. The goal is to write down everything you can. When you are driving, record a monologue of your day and how you are feeling, what you are going to be doing, goals, worries, everything. Record this onto your phone via video or audio.

When you are in an office or at home, as frequently as possible write down your thoughts at any given moment. All day long.

Put it aside and come back to it several days later. Listen and read your recorded thoughts on that day starting with the morning. You will find that what might have started out as a good mood turned into a negative, pessimistic line of thinking. You might find the reverse happening. You might find very little change in your line of thinking; but if you pay attention, you will notice how other people's words, actions, or lack thereof influence your thoughts daily. DAILY.

This is why it is important to establish habits and goals that can be followed with little thought. By not trusting your thoughts so much, you will find drastic improvement in your emotions and mood.

*Live life with intention
rather than by emotion.*

Awareness alleviates pressure. Getting outside of your tendency to over-identify with your thoughts and feelings allows you to live life with intention rather than living by emotion.

PERSONAL REFLECTIONS

- Are you able to observe your thoughts as they randomly enter your mind?

- What thoughts do you hold about yourself that may not be true?

- Make a note of one way that your actions influence your thoughts in your personal life.

- What fearful thoughts have you had that turned out to be untrue or worries that did not come to pass?

- What is the title of the last book you read? (Not this one.)

CHAPTER TWO

ACCEPTANCE AND ACTION

If you correct your mind, the rest of your life will fall into place.—Lao Tzu

To choose your better perspective, first start by becoming aware of the power that your perspective holds in how your, for example, career, relationships, health, hobbies, and your outlook unfold in your life. Learn how the way you view a situation influences your actions and the results of any interaction or set of circumstances that you encounter. When you can see and understand intellectually the power of perspective, you are on your way to achieving whatever you can imagine. This knowledge is the first step toward being able to control and alter your perspective.

Second, learn from others and about yourself by observing behavior and language in each interaction. It's simple: pay attention. Listen to the language that people use when they approach a task or an order of business for the day—are they successful in their approach, or are they failing. You can learn much from observing both outcomes.

Listen to the way you talk to and with your children, your partner, friends, and coworkers. How do you view getting ready in the morning? Do you see it as a hassle? Or do you look forward to it? Beginning to notice your behavior and interactions with people will give you a wealth of information about how your different perspectives affect outcomes. You will also learn a lot about other people in that you will begin to understand why they react the way they do—what their perspectives are. This will help you interact successfully as an employee, supervisor, coworker, parent, spouse, sibling, etc.

POLITICS OF PERSPECTIVE

Critical to this journey is the understanding that no two people on this planet share identical perspectives on everything. In fact, each individual experiences a different world, a different life altogether no matter how close in physical reality they are to each other. Understanding the implications of these differences will help you navigate through workplace politics, family drama, and sticky social situations in general.

If you try to project your perspective on others based on what you think you know about them, you will probably run into frustration and misunderstanding. Also, if you try to persuade or force another person to see things the way you do, you will only cause resentment.

NO ONE SEES THE WAY YOU DO

Recognize and realize, understand and accept the fact that no one sees anything exactly like you do. So often we cause ourselves problems by wanting or trying to get another person to see an issue the way we do. It's impossible, especially when it is a controversial issue or subject that provokes an emotional response.

Instead of trying to persuade, think about inviting people into an experience. It's not about getting them to see your point of view of the experience. Sure you want them to enjoy the experience or the thing or idea that you see so clearly; you want them to enjoy it as much as you do. But, they may or may not. Don't demand anyone to see things the way you do. Rather, share your view with kindness and welcome them to enjoy the things you enjoy—in their own way, from their own perspective.

WHEN TO CHANGE CIRCUMSTANCES INSTEAD OF PERSPECTIVE

The two most important questions that come to my mind when I consider the idea of choosing perspective is, *What limits does this power have? There must be a time when changing my situation is a better move than looking at it differently, right?*

Let's consider.

By looking at your circumstances differently, you will more likely come to conclusions not only about when it is time to change, but also in what ways and by what methods. This doesn't always come when you are lost in negativity or when you are complaining or thinking of how you should have done things differently to avoid being in your current situation.

Change in perspective is the impetus for change in circumstances.

So you see, the change in perspective is the impetus for the change in circumstances. Look at all the people who stay in horrible relationships—whether marital, friendships, or work-related—and never take the necessary steps to get out of those destructive relationships and give themselves the opportunity to find something more beneficial. It's sad. It is a problem of perspective. Whatever their perspective is that allows them to remain in negative but escapable situations—this outlook is the problem. They are not looking at the situation in a way in which they can harness the power that perspective could bring to them.

Can you say the following to yourself and believe it? *I am content with the life I am living and the choices I am making. My decisions may not always be correct, but I trust my motives and I am at peace with who I am.*

If in doubt, ask yourself questions along this line of thought. Your reaction will tell you the truth about your level of dissatisfaction or more importantly, your level of inauthenticity. Are you living in a constant state of cognitive dissonance that comes from your actions contradicting your values and desires? If so, I encourage you to seriously consider your perspective and make the necessary changes so you can be truly content with your life and know you are making wise choices to bring peace.

REDUCE OVERTHINKING

We all have our moments when we overthink a situation or a decision. In many cases, we may even *know* that we are overthinking it, but that still does not give us the answer we want or need. Stay present to avoid overthinking. Making this change in perspective is always possible, no matter in what situation you find yourself. If you are nervous, scared, or overthinking the moments that lie ahead of you, bring yourself back to the present moment by simply looking at a spot on the wall, a feature of nature, or a photo in your phone.

Changing your perspective can be done by concentrating on the way your hand feels as it rests on the arm of the chair or on your desk. It can be accomplished by feeling each step of your feet as you walk across a floor or parking lot or grass. The key is to change your perspective from mental to physical, past to present, or future to present.

Overthinking causes us to not do the thing we need to do to get rid of the doubt, nervousness, or whatever negative emotion we might be feeling.

Stop the self-doubt because it is, as Sylvia Plath points out, the "worst enemy to creativity."

When we evaluate an action or a plan past the point of usefulness, we become paralyzed when movement is most imperative.

How do we get to this point of knowing when we are overanalyzing and then take action to overcome it? Essentially, how do we change perspective on a situation where we are spending too much time in doubt? The following are three ideas to help with the change in perspective that leads to action on an idea:

1. *Think* of the time being wasted by over analysis, of the worst-case scenario (can you survive it?), of the validity of the idea itself (are you capable of seeing it through to completion before deeming it bad based on self-doubt).

2. *Trust yourself* to make the decision you believe is best for the moment and situation you are in with the information you have access to.

3. *Take the action* that comes most naturally to you. Often this is the first inclination or instinct. Not always though. The important thing is to feel some level of comfort even if your mind is not 100 percent in agreement with your action.

The next time you suspect you might be overthinking a decision, run through this mental checklist and proceed accordingly to get yourself out of this time-consuming trap of the mind.

LET GO OF THE NEED TO CONTROL

Much of what keeps people in their negative perspective of the world can be traced back to their desire to control what cannot be controlled. This need for control leads to unrealistic expectations, resulting in disappointment. We will look at ways to bypass or overcome this desire so that we can let go and free our minds to see life's situations from different angles.

Choose your perspective and let go of control over what you do not and cannot control. This is not an argument about free will versus determinism, but simply an observation that it is not rational to imagine you have so much power over life. If you look around, a million things are happening, have happened, could happen, will happen—and there is nothing you can do to change those events in any way.

But wanting to be in control is natural. It takes a change in perspective to realize that others can do a good job, can take on responsibility, are able to decide what is best. Knowing we are not in control of every minute detail of everyday life means that everything is as it is and that there is no reason to get upset and worry and berate ourselves. Instead, if we are in a tight spot, we can think clearly and patiently about what to do to get out of our own way. To delegate or step back and let others who know more about a subject lead the project or make the decision.

AVOID THE VICTIM MENTALITY

The victim mentality is the view that people are out to get you. It's the idea of being easily and frequently offended, many times without the offenders knowing they did anything. People with this mentality trade on the attention of the sympathetic instead of taking personal responsibility for the role they might have played in all perceived or actual offenses.

To understand how detrimental the victim mentality is, you have to take stock of what it costs you. If you are playing the role of the martyr, the perfect person who never hurts anyone's feelings or insults anyone in any way, yet somehow you are still being hurt and offended, then you are sacrificing your goals and dreams that can only be realized by taking personal responsibility for your actions. Taking personal responsibility includes evaluating your feelings and responses to insults or offenses. This might include confrontation. If you aren't able to work it out with the other person involved, maybe it means going your separate ways. Or if you are unwilling to confront the other person about it, then it may mean the offense was not so serious and you need to move on.

Your words and energy affect how you experience life.

Many times, moving on is the best course of action. If you are constantly dwelling on and talking about others' treatment of you, you probably aren't controlling your perspective—rather, you are allowing a lot of negativity into your mind and negative words that you put out into the universe. The words and energy you contribute to the world affects how you experience life.

Being a victim means giving up control of your perspective and hoping to gain validity through the sympathetic perspective of someone else.

CONTROL YOUR CONSUMPTION

Good advertising and marketing ploys are used to breed discontent, to "create an anxiety relievable by purchase" as the late writer David Foster Wallace put it.

In order to control your impulses and moods, you have to overcome this instant-gratification pressure by limiting your television intake and ignoring the persistent and invasive ads on your computer and phone screens. Also, limit the amount of time you spend on social media, and limit the influence that aggregated societal fears and discourse have on your daily activities.

If you allow the fearmongering and sensationalism of the mainstream news media to invade your mind, it can overwhelm and possibly lead to depression. It can aggravate you. It can scare you. All of these things inhibit your ability to think clearly and you need clarity in order to choose your most beneficial perspective. Once you let emotion in, it is much more difficult to maintain a calm state of mind.

Entertainment aside, you still have plenty of drama in the real world of human interaction.

DEALING WITH FAMILY DRAMA

The mental and emotional toll of family drama can be mitigated by understanding on an intellectual level the complicated dynamics of any and every family. Imagine the layers of emotion involved with the psychology of birth order, individual personalities, spouse's personalities and backgrounds, and then add family traditions, religion, parents' personalities and backgrounds, and children and sibling's individual personalities.

By understanding these numerous layers and variables, you can take everything that occurs lightly rather than becoming instantly insulted or hurt. Let go of family baggage and disputes—they are always going to happen, hopefully more infrequently as you grow older. The reality is realizing that family is a combination of unique individuals who lived (or currently live) in the same house, and all your experiences at home with your siblings and your parents, perhaps grandparents and aunts and uncles too, add up to the way you see and handle family and other relationships today.

Let go of family baggage and disputes—they are inevitable.

If divorce, death of a parent(s), or separation was part of your childhood, it can be even more complicated. Or there may have been preferential treatment given to one sibling. Maybe it was you who was favored. Maybe there was a rivalry within the family between sisters or brothers or uncles or parents, etc. Try to see each situation with the perspective of understanding the complicated dynamics of your family and be forgiving, or at least patient. It is highly likely, given the variety of circumstances, that family relationships will be challenging.

If you are part of a family who get along well and with whom you can converse with and enjoy a few hours together on weekends and holidays and help each other out in life, you are blessed. Consider your family a success if you are not always fighting or if you still all speak to each other in a friendly manner and stay in touch. Many families are not so lucky and it is no wonder why. Grasp the truth behind the incredibly complicated dynamics of relationships in today's society and you will be on the way to adopting a perspective of grace when dealing with your family.

CHANGE YOUR PHYSICAL
VANTAGE POINT

A simple way to change your outlook, your perspective, can be to change your current physical position. If you are sitting down, stand up or lie down. If you are reclining, sit up or stand up. Move to a different corner of the room. Move to the center of the room. Stand on a chair or a stepstool and look around from higher ground. Go outside and walk to a place you've rarely stood.

Now look around you. Look at all the familiar objects in your living room, your office, your yard, or the parking lot where your car is parked. It is interesting how, though familiar, things look a little different from different vantage points. Simplistic as it might seem, these little hacks can do wonders for stimulating your mind to essentially do the same thing with your thoughts.

Wrestling with decisions might cause a physical reaction where you typically pace around a room. Or maybe you have some nervous tic like chewing your nails or maybe you doodle incessantly at your desk while you think. When you want to think differently, mix it up by moving from where you are or where you usually would be when indecisive situations occur. Let your mind be open to change in perspective by initiating a physical change in perspective.

FITNESS AND DIET

For me, adopting a perspective of never giving up on my fitness goals has been beneficial to me in the following ways. Although exercising is usually not my first choice of activity or way to spend my time, I don't go too many days without feeling the mental urge to exercise. This is because I have ingrained in my mind the perspective of persistence in fitness.

Even when I go without exercising or when my diet is full of fast food and other poor choices, I don't say, "Ah, forget it," and let myself go. Eventually, I go for a walk and this usually leads to a walk the next day and the next. Then I might lift some weights, which leads to another couple of days of making better food choices and prepping healthy meals instead of going on the fly and just getting food when I'm hungry without prior thought.

You don't want your later-in-life perspective to include regret.

Another hack is to imagine yourself later in life and what you might consider important when you don't have as many years left. When you are young, it is easy to throw caution to the wind when it comes to diet and fitness choices; but remember, the effects of those choices will kick in as you enter into your later years—and many times the effects are irreversible. It is tempting to think that you won't care by that time as you will have lived a long and full life (hopefully), but remember that you will have different perspectives at that stage of life. You don't want those perspectives to include regret about the way you treated your body in your early years.

Of course, I'm not the best source for fitness and diet perspectives—adopt your own perspective that works for you. It is a highly personalized journey you are on when it comes to physical health. Your perspective on your body and how tuned in you are with that perspective will give you the motivation and the strength to keep going after and achieving your fitness goals. The main thing is to figure out a plan of exercise that works for you and stick with it—whether you want to or not!

MUSIC

Music can change your mood, inspire you, and motivate you. Use music for these reasons as much as you can. Music makes the world go around, it's been said, and I believe this to be true. Look at businesses that play upbeat music in the background while you shop and notice that the vibe of the place is generally high energy and positive. Whereas in some businesses where no music is playing, there is solemnness and a lower energy and enthusiasm among the employees—and patrons.

Music can be a great companion when you are working on tedious tasks. Use it to your advantage when you are trying to complete something that you are not necessarily looking forward to finishing. Music can become an aspect of the task that you look forward to hearing, which makes the doing and completing easier. Music is a very healthy way of altering your consciousness. There are many different and *healthy* ways to alter your consciousness, to see from a different perspective. For example: traveling to other regions or countries, or even just researching other countries on the Internet; volunteering at a food bank or animal rescue organization; taking a modern art class or any instruction in a subject that interests you; working on a humanitarian outreach in an impoverished neighborhood; trying a new type of food once a week, etc. Anything that takes you out of your daily routine will change your perspective and widen your world.

WHAT ARE YOU EATING?

This is not a diet book and I am not a medical professional, but there are aspects of diet that anyone can observe and take advantage of when it comes to altering your perspective. When you eat a ton of food, you feel sleepy and sluggish. When you eat greasy food from a burger joint, you may feel the discomfort of stomach pain. Now the sluggishness and the discomfort have clouded your perspective in a way. They have become filters through which you experience everything else as the side effects of your diet control your outlook.

At other times, being hungry causes you to be irritable and you have trouble thinking straight.

If you eat vegetables, clean forms of protein like chicken or fish, and you eat in moderation, you will feel more comfortable physically. Feeling good physically lessens any additional effects on your perspective of the world and the moments you are experiencing.

Not eating every meal and going hungry can intensify and alter your perspective. It can make thoughts crystal clear and cause your energy levels to skyrocket. We eat when we are hungry by intuition, but also by habit.

Skipping meals might not sound too inviting. There will be the discomfort of feeling hungry, but it tends to go away after ten or fifteen minutes and that's when you can access a perspective and mind state that is sharp and clear. Not eating can go too far, of course. You have to maintain common sense about eating. If you are feeling physically weak, you need to eat. You don't necessarily want to skip meals every day if you are losing too much weight, etc. Your physical and mental health are primary concerns and should be taken seriously.

Another way to take action that changes perspective is to plan a trip.

TRAVEL TO GAIN A DIFFERENT PERSPECTIVE

Sometimes living in a different culture even for a brief period of time is enough to help you change your perspective. In what way? The first way that comes to mind is that traveling and living in varying environments force you to do things that you've always done, but in *different ways.* Depending on where you go, perhaps you won't have Wi-Fi or an Internet connection. Oftentimes your living space will be much smaller than what you are used to at home.

In these cases, beyond just enjoying the trip or the scenery or in the case of a business trip, just being caught up in the meetings or events of the days, try thinking about what you can do to improvise or make do with the new situation or circumstances as you travel. Maybe your accommodations are not nearly what you expected, requested, or even paid for. Instead of being enraged and getting caught up in trying to right the real or perceived wrongs of the situation, choose the perspective of being aware of what you can do to make the place work for what you need.

There are numerous steps you will take quite naturally in most cases to improve the situation as much as possible.

Typically, we complain about these things we have to do even though they usually make the situation livable if not perfectly fine for our purposes. The next step is to work on *appreciating* the adjusted circumstances—not the exact circumstances, but the steps you took to rectify the situation.

For example, if you prefer writing on a computer or keyboard, but for whatever reason your computer doesn't work, you must write on paper with a pen or pencil. Or maybe the situation is the way you must cook your food, or the food you have available. Maybe you have to share a hotel room with a colleague for a night while on a business trip. Whatever the case may be, learn to fall in love with the variance, with the nuances of the situation, and take that newfound sense of successfully overcoming an undesirable event home with you and use it to accomplish your goals.

YOU GOT WHAT YOU WANTED, BUT...

It is easy to forget that our dreams and goals are realized and achieved gradually, progressively, and very rarely, suddenly. It's when people make the mistake of thinking it will happen suddenly that they get annoyed with the side effects of success in the area in which they are striving. Nothing is always good. There is no utopia, no elixir that will solve all your problems, and so you must understand that the more you find success, you will also find new problems.

Although you still might prefer a more successful life to your previous life, success comes with problems that you hadn't thought of—problems that you did not previously have. The problems will come on gradually, just like your success. Your lifestyle will not change as quickly as you hope or imagine that it might. So, recognizing this truth, understand that the problems you gain are a result of your own actions. They are a direct result of your striving for change.

Own the perspective of being the source of your current situation. Own the idea that it is your life and your chosen path and the path will not always be without obstacles and discomfort.

The sooner you are able to own and accept this perspective in dealing with your minor achievements—each step up the proverbial ladder of success—the better you will be able to handle the setbacks and annoyances that come with these gains.

PERSONAL REFLECTIONS

- In what areas of your life should you take action to change rather than changing your perspective?

- Where in your life can you let go and accept circumstances by seeing them a different way?

- How long has it been since you traveled away from home? What do you remember about that trip?

- Are you a healthy eater? How could you improve your diet and exercise habits this week?

- When do you use music to influence your perspective?

CHAPTER THREE

POSITIVITY

"There are two ways of spreading light—
to be the candle or the mirror that reflects it."
—Edith Wharton

It is critical to gain the skill of finding a positive perspective regardless of your circumstances. There may be nothing more important in your journey to accomplishing your goals. If you do not find the positive spin, you will waste time in despair and take actions that lead to even more unfavorable circumstances and conditions.

The training of your mind to find the optimistic side of daily life is not a difficult task to complete. It is a matter of repetition. Every day, EVERY DAY, something unfavorable happens to you. Something will happen tomorrow that causes the emotions of anger, sadness, frustration, and or anxiety to well up within. How you respond to the circumstance is what matters most.

Use emotion to trigger your mind and adjust your perspective.

It is okay to feel the stress, anger, or whatever emotion comes to you as a result of that event. The trick is to immediately use the emotion as a trigger to change your mind and adjust your perspective to see the good in it. For example, if your vehicle has an unexpected flat tire on the way to work, but you have a spare and a jack—be thankful that you have the tools to fix the flat and can drive to a garage to have the tire repaired or replaced.

Maybe you *don't* have the spare or the jack, but you have a phone. Appreciate the technology of cell phones that allows you to call a friend, family member, or a tow truck. These are some not-too-serious circumstances and situations in which you can practice controlling your perspective.

When the serious trouble comes, it will be a little easier to find the positive if you have been practicing it with your daily problems.

This is how you can continue to work and pursue your goals and dreams without being derailed by a pessimistic outlook that results in paralysis or half-hearted attempts.

THOUGHTS CREATE EMOTIONS

On the days when the snowball of negative thoughts is formed and begins to roll down the hill picking up more and more negativity and becoming exponentially bigger, what else happens? What else happens to a snowball as it gets bigger and bigger? Not only does it take up more space, it also gets heavier.

Just like that, negative thoughts that could have passed quickly through our minds and out are collected and begin to stick together and create a weight within our minds. This weight gets heavier and heavier and soon all we can think about is the weight, and nothing outside of it can get our full attention. Anything outside of our weight, our snowball, becomes an aggravating distraction to our actual problems that need to be solved.

Our fuse becomes shorter and we find ourselves getting angry easily, which of course creates circumstances and thoughts and actions that add to the existing weight. The emotions created by the thoughts are the weights, and it is not as easy to drop the emotions as it is to drop the thoughts.

How do we break free? There are several all-to-common experiences that every person has to deal with almost daily. Let's examine each one and determine to overcome every self-defeating perspective.

BAD MOOD

When you are in a bad mood—regardless of why—but for the sake of example, let's say it is a rainy, cold day and you woke up feeling low and not even coffee is helping you shake the blues. Here are some quick ways to force your perspective somewhat.

Smile. Force yourself to smile. First, smile into a mirror at yourself. It will feel goofy, but hold it there until the smile becomes natural—and it will because you will feel ridiculous and then you'll be unable to contain that smile. Then you'll find yourself smiling at others as well and your perspective will lose some of the unnecessary weight.

Jump up and down. Jumping jacks or whatever, but jump around and get your feet off the ground and lose that negative energy by way of changing your physical activity in a drastic manner. Push-ups or sit-ups work just as well, but I like the idea of jumping as it is something more childish and prone to make you forget your gloomy perspective.

Laugh out loud. This works for the same reason the smile does. It's infectious.

Go for a run. If time and physical condition allow, going for a run or swift walking increases endorphins and allows your mind to circulate thoughts and come up with a different arrangement, perspective, by the end.

BAD HABITS

Many of our bad habits can be overcome by replacing them with a more constructive or positive action. The trick is to learn how to look forward to the replacement more than the bad habit. Start with one day at a time rather than saying, "For the next week, I will...." Keep your commitment to a day at a time. "Today, I will replace my bad habit with a good habit."

For many years, I struggled with habit replacement because I would make my goal too hard to reach for my state of mind. It was demoralizing to not be able to go a full week or a month, depending on the habit and goal. Although exercise and diet are hard habits to incorporate into many people's lifestyle, we naturally want to think that we can make it for a week or two weeks. But when we don't, the damage is done.

Our confidence is delated and our perspective begins to skew negatively toward our capabilities. Our minds begin to tell us that our habits are worse than what they are or we start to label ourselves in negative ways.

Just commit to one day at a time. We can make it one day on that diet or exercise program or simply taking a walk. Start with one day, then eventually you will build your stamina and confidence to increase that length of time to replace your bad habit for a good one.

HANDLING CRITICISM

What's more challenging than maintaining a steady, optimistic attitude after you or your work has been criticized? Criticism can sting. Criticism can cause you to get angry, depressed, or even quit working on your goals.

There are ways to maintain a calm, clear perspective even after being criticized. Think about what it means to feel judged. When someone says something negative about your work or your ideas or even something as simple as your clothing, you first have to agree that the comment is right in order to feel hurt.

The next time this happens, try the following:

- Observe and release your initial emotional reaction

- Consider the criticism's merit

- Decide to act upon it or ignore and move on

When your ego feels attacked, emotion is triggered and your assessments and thinking begin to lack clarity. It is important to consciously push your emotional reactions to the side so you can get to the end of the process and keep your thoughts clearly on your goals and what you are trying to accomplish in the big picture.

Considering the validity of the criticism—if there is any—is important for growth. There may be some truth in the critical statements made about you or your work. How can you address the issues and improve? How can you make it so those criticisms are not made again or not as often?

You are your own judge.

An important note: many people discount criticism immediately because they don't like the person offering it. This can be a mistake. When you remove emotion from the thought process, you will see only the ideas and then you can weigh them on their own merit without personal feeling toward the person putting the ideas forward.

Regardless of whether there is validity to the criticizer's words or not, the next step is to move on and get back to achieving your goals based on your own perspective of yourself and your worth. Ultimately, judgment is made by you—and if you can remember this, you will spend less time worrying about trying to make everyone else happy and more time working on what you do best.

At other times, people will offend you either inten-tionally or unintentionally and we have to manage our emotions in those situations.

OFFENSE

When someone says or does something that offends you, you might be tempted to lash out or avoid them poten-tially. Remember that your ideal of self-importance is often one of the strongest inhibitors of a well-lived life. To live life fully,

Don't focus on petty stuff that won't matter in the morning.

open yourself to the world just as you open your mind to thoughts and creative ideas.

When you go around with hurt feelings, it mostly hurts you. It slows down your progress toward attaining your goals. There will always be reasons to be offended and hurt when dealing with fellow human beings; and depending on the offense, it may be appropriate to react or confront. But be careful not to focus on the petty stuff—the kind of insults that may or may not have been intentional, the kind of things that really won't matter in the morning.

How do you alter your perspective on perceived offenses? Make a decision to release it. Decide to address the offense or let it go. Usually, you can let it go. Don't revisit it or rehash it with someone else, just release it and move on with your day.

It's easier to make this wise decision each time, and you'll feel better, get more done, and see a brighter world when choosing this perspective regarding offenses.

DAILY DREARINESS

Turn dreary, mundane tasks into games. Compete with yourself. For example, if you're loading freight onto a truck or numbers into the computer and have always done it a certain way, try something new and keep track of the time. You may surprise yourself! Or if you always drive the same route to work or school, try a different way to change up the monotony of the daily drive time and see if you save or add a few minutes.

Or, compete with another person who has a similar task and perspective. My brother told me the story of when he and his friend passed the time as cashiers at a grocery store by establishing a set of rules for a game. They would compete to see who could ring up and bag customers' groceries the fastest. They had lots of laughs and fun in what could've been a boring job.

NOT A MORNING PERSON

If it's true that you are not a morning person, consider a change in your perspective about that time of day. I know there is some inherent or nurtured preference for certain times of the day when we may be more productive and relaxed, but many times we take the social conditioning of dreading Monday mornings for the popular joke fodder that it is for people who are dissatisfied with their jobs or work.

There are things to be enjoyed about the morning though. Find those things and focus on them.

Beyond this, start working on eliminating the cliché comments about not being a morning person or any other typical comment about going to work in the morning being a negative experience. Replace those statements with phrases of gratitude. Find positivity for the situation you are in and speak those words more often than negativity.

CONTROLLING PERSPECTIVE IN PERSONAL CRISIS

Are you facing the loss of your job, the end of a relationship, legal or financial problems? Whatever the case, there is a way to maintain your perspective of optimism and opportunity during these undesirable and potentially even miserable times of stress and worry.

There are many different situations in our society and lives that could cause the sort of grief and distress that cause nervous breakdowns or paralysis when we need to be calm more than ever.

Especially when we are not used to trauma, danger, or stress in life, the ability to stay coolheaded can be very hard to grasp.

But regardless, a level-headed, productive mindset can be achieved during times of personal crisis. The following are a few steps when faced with a situation that has you so worked up that you can't think straight and can't relax and see things clearly:

1. Take slow, deep breaths and understand that you are okay in the current moment. If you are physically conscious and alive, then you have the ability to come to this realization that at least for the moment, the world is not ending. This is an important first step.

2. Let go of control. If the impending crisis, or present crisis—say, loss of job or loss of a loved one—is something that you cannot change, the next step is to let go of the illusion of control. You do not control this situation. When you let go of that pressure to try to change something, you will find yourself calming down. Let go.

3. Evaluate the situation and decide what you *do* control. After your heart rate has slowed and your nervous system is returning to normal, take time to

write down the aspects of the crisis in which you can exert some action to cause change or to improve your present situation. That may be something as basic as taking a walk or exercising to release some of that built-up nervous energy. It may be phone calls to trusted friends or a support system. Or maybe it is something more precise like setting up an appointment with an attorney, etc. Find out what you can do, and intentionally proceed to do it. One step at a time.

4. Throughout the ordeal, stay focused on the *now* as much as possible. There may be times when you need to look ahead to schedule a meeting or a phone call, but resist the urge to look back and think about what you could have done differently. The past is over and trying to go back will only further inhibit your progress of gaining the perspective you need to move through the current personal crisis and come out okay on the other side.

5. Talk to someone you trust. This someone should be a person who has successfully weathered a personal crisis, but not necessarily. The main characteristic is that you trust this person's advice, in most cases, more than anyone else's. But if you don't have such a person in your life, you can still control your perspective in a crisis—read the first four steps again.

Try some or all of these steps the next time you find yourself in a crisis situation and want to control your outlook so you can make the right decisions to get through it as quickly as possible. You will learn something valuable about yourself in the process.

IT WILL PASS

Always remember that "It will pass" when you have an absolutely horrible day. You might have heard this saying so many times that it seems only cliché and not worth consideration. But this saying is repeated to the point of cliché because it is true.

The idea that it will pass is a simple reminder to deploy gratitude whenever you feel like your situation is less than desirable. There is always something to complain about and sometimes there are more things than less; but remember, it is always true that someone has it much worse. Successful entrepreneur Gary Vaynerchuk puts it this way, "Whatever you complain about, your grandparents had it worse."

You could be sitting in the county jail, a homeless shelter, or living on

"Whatever you complain about, your grandparents had it worse."

PERSONAL REFLECTIONS

- What part of your daily activities triggers your negative thoughts?

- What bad habits can you eliminate to increase your positivity?

- How do you handle being criticism or disagreement?

- Do you notice how your thoughts influence your emotions?

the streets with no money, no food, and no hope. There are people in those conditions right now as you read this, so if you can imagine the negative side effects of those situations, go ahead and compare them to your own and be thankful. You have hope. Now own this perspective and make the best out of your situation today, because the bad times *will* pass!

CHAPTER FOUR

PRODUCTIVITY

Do the thing and you shall have the power.
—Ralph Waldo Emerson

PLAN YOUR DAY; PREPARE YOUR PERSPECTIVE

Planning and prioritizing your day influences your perspective in several ways. Number one, it forces you to consider the day in light of your goals. Number two, it helps you to feel prepared the night before. I recommend planning your day the night before rather than in the morning, but do what works for you.

Plan right down to the outfit you are going to wear, the food you will consume, and the tools you need for your work. Have everything ready and packed the night before as much as possible. Have your outfit washed and ironed and ready to put on first thing in the morning. For the extra bit of work in the evening, you will have free mental space and a more upbeat perspective when you wake up knowing that you are ready to go.

With planning also comes the opportunity for your mind to recognize and act on possibilities that would not have been recognized when the mind is consumed with the mundane activities of getting ready for the day. Ideas, new ideas, potentially profitable ideas are noticed when the mind is free from worry or other thoughts of the daily necessities like packing a lunch or finding an outfit to wear.

A bit of evening work = freer mental space in the morning.

Have your priority list of tasks ready the night before and review when you are ready to begin work in the morning. Again, your perspective will be positive, more free and ready to be creative throughout your day than if you are racing around in hasty preparation.

CONCENTRATION THROUGH ACTION

How long can you do one thing without your mind wandering far enough way that it causes you to forget what you were doing? How many hours can you sit without doing anything other than what you sat down to do, whether write, read, sew, or repair something?

Concentration through action is the secret to having a different perspective on work. It is taking the action that leads to the ideas and inspiration.

Imagine approaching writing as writing what you think rather than thinking about what you write. Do you notice the differ-

> *Taking action leads to ideas and inspiration.*

ence? Try it sometime. It is amazing what can be accomplished and how our minds can be changed by *doing* something, and then paying attention to the thoughts that come as a result.

Instead, we think about everything and try to know each step of the way before we start out. Sometimes this is important, but many times it is not. Take action and see what happens. Make sure to pay special attention to the thoughts that arise, the aura, the surrounding energy you feel when you are in the process of doing what you set out to do. Do the things you only thought about up to this point, then notice how your perspective has changed about them.

What I hope you will begin to notice is an ability to stay with the task at hand due to a lack of thinking about anything else. It is the joy of *doing* rather than thinking that leads to concentration. Concentration is often seen as a hard thing to do, something difficult—but it can be effortless. It can come about organically from the doing of your work.

Success in life is a mental game, and a big part of it is concentrating the attention.

CREATE YOUR OBSESSION— A BURNING DESIRE

I used to mistake burning desire as a passion or as something that needed to be found, but now I recognize that my burning desire is something that I *do*. Something that I've done—and it may be something that I've gotten away from and have not done in a week, a month, or maybe even years, but it is inherent and it is not to be escaped without consequence.

You might ask, "Well, how is *finding* different from *recognizing* in this case?"

Finding implies something being lost or something that is apart and needs to be located, whereas recognizing implies known and familiar. Compare the feeling of looking for someone you have not met (maybe a business contact at the airport) and, on the other hand, unexpectedly seeing your good friend in a crowd. This visual might help if you are wondering what your obsession is and imagining it if you don't have one.

A *healthy obsession* keeps you steady in the unsteady nature of life and gives your life a meaning that cannot be taken from you. If it is a useful obsession, it will take you far and let you experience life with its brightness and opportunities more pronounced.

Everybody, including you, has something special that makes them "tick"—a way of looking at life, including the field or industry you are interested in, your goals, your family, etc. Whatever the case, there is some area of interest in your life that can be turned into a healthy obsession, igniting a burning desire. Practice being aware in your daily existence and you will recognize the opportunity to create an obsession.

When your obsession becomes greater than your ego, then you've reached another level in choosing your perspective. You are free from the criticism of others, free from the fear of other people's minds. When you are obsessed with something, you don't have time to hear or imagine what others, or your ego, might be saying.

What is your obsession? What *could* be your obsession? It doesn't have to be one thing; it can be many different things. The idea of obsession can be a mental approach to everything that you do. When you come to tasks with an obsessive mindset, it means you are working on that task to the exclusion of all else. Being obsessed means you are present with that task and the work involved, and you are willing to seek out solutions to problems and not give up.

Of course, there is a fine line between an unhealthy obsession, or being overzealous, that you must be keen to acknowledge. Taking anything to the extreme can be detrimental to your mental, emotional, relational, and physical welfare. But an obsessive personality *can* be a great way to show up in life. When it comes to family life and spending time with your partner or friends, obsession can manifest as not working on your phone or texting when you are present with them. Being obsessed is giving your whole, undivided attention to the person or people you are with for the entire time you are with them.

The perspective of having a healthy obsession can lead to fulfillment through working harder and being more present in each moment of your experience.

FOCUS ON THE DETAILS

Many times, we like to look at the big picture. We like to look at or imagine the results of what we are *planning* to do rather than really zooming in on and finding joy in the moment-to-moment, sometimes tedious, details of what we are doing. The day-to-day work is what brings us to the big picture, the ultimate goal, and the day-to-day detail work is what we spend most of our time doing, whether we like it or not. Period.

This truth often gets lost in translation and fantasy. It's fun to fantasize and consider what life could be like or what the feelings of accomplishment might actually feel like if such and such scenario were to occur, or if we were to achieve this goal or another—but fantasy alone will not take us there.

The minute-to-minute existence makes up our lives. Too many times, we focus on five-year goals and seven-year plans instead of learning to love and enjoy the everyday steps of the big plan. All it takes is a different way of looking at the tedium. Find joy in the mundane. Find energy and motivation in boredom. While it may sound counterintuitive—it is possible and it is rewarding and it is the way to finding joy in the details.

Really look at and pay attention to what you are doing on a daily basis, especially during those times when you are inconvenienced for whatever reason. Notice that if you slow down just a bit, you might have fun doing what you do. Not just fun, but actual and gratifying satisfaction. Note the satisfactory feelings you have when you are knocking out tasks that need to be done. The emotions of contentment and satisfaction

Love and enjoy the everyday steps of the big plan.

are available, just be aware and change your perspective about what you thought was boring and mundane. Soon, you will start looking forward to the daily grind. It's true—try it.

FIND OPPORTUNITY IN CHAOS

A quote from Sun Tzu's famous book, *The Art of War*, states, "In the midst of chaos, there is also opportunity." You can find opportunity to make progress on your goals or to find some seed of a creative idea in the middle of an unfortunate or a maddening, frustrating, angering, or even stressful situation. This is the perspective that has distinguished leaders and set warriors above the pack. It does the same for everyone who chooses to seize every chaotic situation and turn it into a productive component of the whole.

The ability to find calmness in craziness is nothing more than the ability to control our perspective. Controlling perspective in chaos is possible to attain through several methods. One is to own the mantra of staying calm no matter the external conditions and making that come true through sheer will power during times of distress.

Controlling your perspective in chaos is possible!

Another method is to enter the chaos intentionally as a way of looking forward to the battle so you can test your resolve and fortitude. In less metaphorical terms, when life is busy as hell, stay in the center of it. Do not try to escape through your normal, conflict-avoiding means. Stay with it, stay engaged. This is a perspective more than an action. The action will certainly follow the perspective, but it is simply a way of looking at something that is often seen as negative in a positive light.

No calm, no rest in your personal life right now? These last few weeks, months, or even years have been nothing but stressful? Okay, get in the mix and see what you can get done professionally. See what you can learn about yourself. See what you can create from the pain.

What side projects have you put off for one reason or another? Dive back in. It's true that some of the best art has been created from places of pain. This is because instead of wallowing in their misery, artists found opportunities for productivity in the midst of chaos and pain. They chose their perspective.

PROSPERITY PERSPECTIVE

Examine your lifestyle and notice the prosperity. Take time to think about the opportunities to grow, build, and create a better life if you choose to do so. Be thankful for your mind and the miracle that you are alive and enjoying this experience called life.

If you are not enjoying it, what are you focusing your mind on? Do you spend your days thinking about how unfair life has been to you because of the pain you live with? No matter how rough your life has been up to this point, appreciate the fact that you are alive. You have opportunities to change your life, but you won't notice them if you are only looking through a lens of lack. When you look through the cloudy lenses of your problems, you can't see the light of life all around you.

Choose your perspective by acknowledging the prosperous aspects of your life. Begin to take action to change your lenses by taking advantage of the opportunities around you instead of talking and thinking about what is wrong. This may be hard because you are in the habit of seeing the worst, but it really is worth the change in perspective—you will find yourself smiling more and having more friends and actually enjoying waking up in the morning, excited to see what the day brings.

BE DOING, NOT TALKING

Burn it into your mind to be the one doing, not talking. It is so easy and common to discuss ideas, the merit and practicality of said ideas, the money-making potential, and possible pitfalls. It's easy to speculate about how much time it would take to execute each of these ideas, the drawbacks of that timeline, and the cost of beginning the process. And so on and so forth.

Of course, there must be some planning if you are about to embark on a business venture of some sort or if you are about to quit your job to begin a home-based business. But be aware that it is a common trap to get stuck in the planning phase and never move forward to take action.

Don't get stuck in the planning phase.

Keep an eye on how much work you are getting done. If you're not even doing what you could be doing without further planning, you could be making the mistake of getting caught up in the trap of over-talking an idea.

Take action today!

IGNORING THE ATTRACTION OF DISTRACTION

Distraction comes in a million different forms. Be aware and be ready to react to distractions when they come. Your reaction is your chosen perspective on whatever distraction is before you. Some distractions are not obvious and you may not realize your ability to choose a perspective on them when they first arise.

Common distractions include:

- Checking the time.

- Looking at your phone.

- Stopping to think about lunch or dinner.

- Wondering about family situations.

- Coworkers coming by to chat.

- Getting another cup of coffee.

- Hearing or feeling the alert set on your phone for a text message, email, or a voicemail.

Are you okay with how often you check your phone? Are you okay with coworkers interrupting you? Most of these distractions are almost involuntary actions. They are habits. When habits become distractions, then you are losing control over them. By control, I mean the ability to consciously recognize your behavior and change.

Evaluate the distractions you allow into your daily life. Decide whether you want to do something to limit or eliminate them or if you are okay with certain forms. This is how you control and choose your perspective on distractions.

Once you begin to strengthen your ability to concentrate, overcome distractions, and produce more work for your efforts, your perspective will become sharp and focused, ready for the challenges of achieving your goals.

PERSONAL REFLECTIONS

- How does your personal productivity affect your perspective?

- How does your perspective affect your productivity?

- What distracts you the most?

- How would you rate your ability to concentrate?

- What are you obsessed with?

- What idea should you take action on?

CHAPTER FIVE

PATIENCE

Because of impatience we were driven out of Paradise,
because of impatience we cannot return.—W.H. Auden

Much is made of time. We mark and measure our lives by the idea of time. When aspiring to reach goals, it is important to work at your own pace and to own your perspective of time. There are subtle differences—and some not so subtle—in the way each person considers time. Notice how some people seem to be perpetually late, while others place extreme value and importance on being early to appointments, meetings, or wherever they are expected to be.

Then there are times when we have to compromise our view of time to match another person's view, and we also have to have a level of respect for other people's views of time. Understanding that we all see time differently is the beginning choosing your perspective on your pace of living and accomplishing.

When we compare our own achievements and accomplishments to others, we lose an appropriate perspective. In a way, everyone lives in different time zones. Just because someone has completed goals that you would like to complete, does not make that person more or less successful than you—just on a different timing.

Success and time are personal. Keep your perspective full of your own goals to achieve on your own timeline. Give yourself grace and keep working.

JUST A STEPPING STONE

Sometimes we get hung up on thinking that if we are working in a job we think is below our standard or that we feel is less than what we are capable of doing, that somehow indicates failure. It's not. Choose your perspective by seeing your current job as a learning experience.

Don't forget where you are, but continue working toward other goals.

I like to think of careers and jobs as stepping stones or rungs on a ladder. Each one is a stage or chapter in our lives, which are full of opportunities for growth if we will notice and take advantage of them.

Your occupation is not permanent. You never know what could happen tomorrow, you could lose your job or career or business. Always work toward another step, another option in your life. This will bring you satisfaction when you feel discontented where you are. Don't get so far into your next chapter that you forget where you are, but do continue working toward other goals. It takes the pressure off you. It eliminates the feelings of needing to "get out of here" or move on to something more fulfilling.

LEAVING THE PAST BEHIND

It's easy to say what is done is done, but what if what is done is still hard to live with? This is when you want to shift your mind, your perspective, back to the now—to this very moment. But how do you bring your thoughts and attention from the past to the present on command?

One method of shifting your perspective is to pay attention to the physical sensations of what you are doing right now. Each second. So for me right this second, I can feel my fingers hitting the keys on the keyboard. I can feel my feet resting on the base of the desk chair. I can feel my elbows resting on the arm of the chair, and

I am watching each word appear out of nowhere onto the screen in front of me.

This is the way to come back to the present. I mentioned this method previously, but it is worth discussing again. Bring in as many details about your present moment as possible. Even if you are ostensibly doing nothing at all beyond reading this book, pay attention to the physical aspects of where and how you are sitting or standing. Maybe you are listening to this book on audio while on the couch with your head on a pillow. Or are you driving? Are you taking a walk? Working out? Washing the dishes?

Whatever the case may be at this moment, notice the smallest detail of what you are doing and what is going on around you. The feel of the steering wheel in your hands, the dishcloth wiping away the spaghetti sauce from the dish. Take interest in this level of detail and you will find that—for the moment, hopefully longer— you've forgotten about the unfortunate past event and the story you had told yourself about it.

DON'T OVERANALYZE OFFENSES

It is not always beneficial to analyze an event after it happens. Be at peace with it and live in the moment. It happens that you can overthink a situation to the point where you make it into something it was not and does not need to be.

Let it be.

Even if it is a situation where you are sure you are in the right and the other person is in the wrong, weigh the cost of escalating it by running through it over and over again in your mind.

The comment, the look, the tone, the email—paranoia. Don't let your mind spiral out of control because of what could be faulty perceptions. Many times there is no need to perceive anything past the initial perception. Just let it go and move forward with a positive and healthy mental and physical life.

The present moment is your only true reality.

Remember, the present moment is your only true reality—not that comment your colleague made to you five minutes ago. Use the power of the present moment to choose your perspective.

It's easy after you do it a few times. You hear something that offends you, but you know it's not something that needs to be addressed, yet you have an overactive mind, or so it seems to you, and you continually replay the conversation and think of the ways in which you could have responded to make things right, to make yourself look strong or smart. Or you wonder what was meant by the comment. But then you choose to change your perspective, and within seconds, you get back to work. You move on to another conversation, you don't bring up the offending person or the remarks, and before you know it, time has passed and you've forgotten all about it. Choose to have a forgiving perspective about people's careless comments and keep moving forward.

EXERCISE YOUR MIND

Moving quickly past an insensitive or offensive comment is a way of controlling perspective and is an excellent example of repetition helping you to get better at a skill. It's not always hard work. Sometimes it is simply repetition. Make a habit of moving on from negative comments or cynical statements from others.

Other times, the hard work is confronting a situation or approaching strangers to tell them about your product—any situation in which your mind must be controlled in order to perform a necessary action. With repeated exposure to the situation, your mind will become stronger and stronger and you will begin to master whatever fear or worry you associate with the task.

LIFE AND DEATH

Speaking of fear, what is your perspective on death? Death is a touchy subject, but it's good to think about and understand what you feel about dying so you can embrace and live with those beliefs.

Of course, for some people there is a sense of unease due to our inherent fear of the unknown. Death has been feared throughout the ages and it will be a fear for us innately as we are wired to survive—but the subject doesn't need to be a dark cloud over our daily lives and our personal goals.

Another reason why it is important to choose your perspective

Coming to grips with death allows us to live life more fully.

on death is that it helps you to remember it is part of being alive. When you make yourself consider what you think about death and how you feel about it, you are reminded of its inevitability. This in turn can be a great motivator. When you know your time alive is finite, life takes on more value. Not only this but there is an underlying sense of urgency to accomplish, do, be, see, and build what you would like to leave behind as your story.

The acceptance of your eventual demise can inspire you to relax and lessen the amount of pressure you put on yourself. It all comes to an end. Knowing this, you can be patient. There is great value in considering our mortality.

The saying, "Live each day as if it were your last" is a valuable line to remember as often as you can.

PROCRASTINATION

If you are prone to procrastination like me, then understand that you will get done what you need to get done when push comes to shove. If you have a strong work ethic, you won't drop the ball. Why is this important to recognize? Because mentally, we tend to judge ourselves irrationally and this leads to us repeating negative thoughts like, *I'm not being very productive today,* or *I haven't accomplished ANYTHING,* or *I'm totally overwhelmed with all this work I have to do!*

The reality is that you might be procrastinating—because you can. You know what you are capable of and you know that when it comes down to the wire, you get it done. Your thoughts can derail you into having a rough day just because you tell yourself it is a rough day. Take a minute and let that sink in.

If you spun the same scenario 180 degrees, you could be enjoying the slower-paced day and the fact that you are in a good position workwise, ahead of the game, instead of lamenting the lack of production or motivation. Be okay with who you are, how you work, and eventually, the temptations of your mind to judge yourself for it.

On the other hand, procrastination can become a problem, but not one without a solution.

There is mental crispness, a well-defined path forward you see when you consciously choose your perspective.

You can overcome procrastination by adopting a view of the task that leads you into it instead of sitting and thinking about it.

Many people think too much about what they need to do, and they know this. But it's not enough to *know* it is a problem, the next step is to find a solution. To find a solution, you have to have a proper perspective of both the problem and possible ways to solve it. So, act on what you know. Start doing what you need to do even if your attitude is negative toward it.

Think about what you are doing in light of your larger goals. Think about what you are doing down to the minutiae of actually doing it. If you are working on a project, try to find yourself looking at each detail, immerse yourself into the work rather than letting yourself sit outside of it "trying to get work done."

Act on what you know.

Your mind opens up when you get inside the obstacle, which is the work that you must complete. The work that you are resisting is the way forward—go inside it instead of around it and you will see. Your perspective will be focused, and you will find that you are no longer procrastinating.

Following the completion of the task you had been putting off, you may realize the time involved was not what you expected, and the task itself was not as painful to complete as you imagined. Now you can choose your perspective on similar tasks in the future.

YOU HAVE TIME

We get in a hurry to accomplish goals and reach milestones by the time we are a certain age or within a certain timeframe, but remember that the days and years and other ways in which we mark time are somewhat arbitrary. Time is a concept, and every individual lives life at their own pace.

Of course, we are forced in the constraints of time in many areas of our life. If you don't show up to work by the time the boss requires you to be there, eventually you may have to find another job. If you don't deliver products to your customers by the time you

promised, you'll lose your customers and your business. If you consistently miss appointments with people
because you are not there at the agreed upon time, you
will lose those clients or connections. These are reali-
ties of our culture, society, and civilization. But outside
of those necessary demarcations of time, patience can
be deployed.

When you don't put pressure on yourself to be somebody
different from who you are, you will find that it's easier
to be patient. When you are patient, you are willing to
put in the long hours of the sometimes tedious work that
is required to reach your goals. When you are looking
at time as something to be beaten or raced against, as
another form of pressure, you increase your chances of
wasting opportunities or missing them because you are
trying for success too quickly. Your expectations are out
of alignment with your abilities or your personality. Or,
you are unwilling to put in the work needed because
of self-judgment, that you should be further along than
you are.

Learn patience. It is indeed such a virtue and a valuable
perspective on living a life of purpose and intentionality.

DON'T THINK OF LOST TIME

This section is a perspective on time as well as language. Try not to make negative statements like, "We lost three days by not having this done!" or similar statements. When we talk like this, not only are we missing the fact that all we have is now, we are putting negative thoughts into our minds and reinforcing the idea of missing something rather than emphasizing the fact that we have everything we need to make the right decision to move forward regarding the issue at hand. There is always a solution, but it won't be found in what is lost.

We work *now* to achieve what we want to achieve and this will carry us through unfortunate circumstances by keeping us focused on what is in front of us, not behind.

FLEXIBILITY OF SCHEDULE AND MENTALITY

Tomorrow is today, yesterday is gone forever. Your perspective on the day dictates your level of stress and weight and ability to be quick and flexible when necessary. If you are living from a place of guilt, need, or self-loathing, you will fall short—and when opportunities come and you must move on them, you will be a few seconds too late.

Learn the concept of *mental elasticity*. Mental elasticity is an idea, when practiced, can:

- Enable you to spin negatives into positives

- Make an unproductive day at work the source of a genius idea

- Allow you to react with no emotion to someone who is angry and taking out their anger on you

- Help you to embrace a contradictory view of time and space and the world

Flexibility of the mind can allow you to create time for yourself.

Being too busy to take a phone call is not a disappointment or a failure of time management, instead it becomes evidence that the idea you are working on is going to pay off because it is consuming your best thoughts—your best time.

An unproductive day at work is such because there is something else your mind is telling you it wants to focus on today. Let yourself be free of self-judgement and calm your mind. Perhaps you will allow the space necessary for the idea you've been waiting for to show itself. The manifestation of this idea may induce productivity in short order.

Looking at the world from a "big picture" perspective can lessen the delusion of self-importance. It can lend an unfocused, peripheral view of your experience that allows you to experience more images, more sensations at once while also recognizing your smallness and reducing the layers of filters that alter your perception of what you experience. Paradoxically, the focusing of the mind upon specific images, tasks, and thoughts in small increments of time gives the perspective a timeless, tight quality, and you, the ability to get lost in your work, to create more than you ever thought possible. It allows you to solve problems and experience the beauty and miracle of life in another way.

NO NEED TO GRIND OR HUSTLE TO ACCOMPLISH MORE

You may be frustrated or deterred by the perspective of hustling 24/7 or working like a maniac around the clock as the only way to get additional work done on your side hustle or your hobby that you hope to turn into a home-based business. Try seeing it from a different perspective. Make a six-month plan for example. You don't need to work fast or constantly to accomplish more work toward various projects.

Use the time you typically throw away. What time do you have in the evenings, mornings, or maybe at lunch time that you could use to put in work on your other endeavors? Again, it's not the speed of your hustle or the number of hours of work, it's the choices you make with how you spend your time. Perspective.

You have plenty of time. And you realize this when you start cutting into the time that you spend sleeping or watching TV. You will find there is still plenty of time left even though you spent an extra hour working.

ARE YOU LIVING YOUR DREAM TODAY?

This question has at its roots two ideas to think about. Number one, we are often so focused on looking forward, focused on achievement and a metaphorical ladder of success, and living our dreams that we sometimes fail to realize we *are* living the life we imagined for ourselves years ago! Sometimes we do not realize it because we are so focused on the *next* dream, the *next* goal, the *next* accomplishment.

There are some ways in which the perspective of always looking forward to the next thing is good and useful and helpful—but when it makes you fail to enjoy the current moments, and when you fail to realize and be grateful for the fact that you are already successful, it's time to reevaluate your perspective in a big way.

The second thing is to look back—just for a moment—and see if the way you are living is part of what was only a dream a few years ago. Is it possible that you have already achieved a certain part of your goal, and if so, are you enjoying this success? Are you stopping to congratulate yourself and thanking those who've helped you and supported you to this point?

Many of us are so forward-focused that we are missing

Celebrate your current success!

out on the best of life, which is right now. It is always right now. Take a moment and celebrate the successes you've experienced and use them as motivation to continue forward.

BE AT PEACE WITH THE MOMENT

To find a sense of stillness and a proper perspective on the problems of life, think of life as only this moment you are in. This "in the moment" thread runs throughout this book for a reason. It is an important aspect of living a wholesome, joyful, and peaceful life. Relax and be as present as possible within the singular moment you are in right now. Notice the sounds, the sensations, the sense of infinity within moment-to-moment existence.

Work with yourself to be able to do this on command. It is useful in bringing your perspective back to one of optimism during times of stress, depression, or frustration. Come back to the moment and gain perspective on the miracle of being alive. The goal is to gain an idea of how small your problems are and to reinvigorate your ambition and drive to succeed and make the best out of the life you've been given.

SET GOALS, BE SPECIFIC, BE CONSISTENT

Make sure your goal is specific. If someone asks you what your goal in life is, have an answer. That answer will be your truth and purpose. It may be your legacy someday. Your goals are your lighthouse in the craziness of life. Keep them front and center when you are the most stressed out in your personal or professional life; maintain a perspective of your goals that won't allow you to forget them.

Don't push your goals aside in favor of stressful issues. Making your goals a priority and not giving up on them will translate into a clearer perspective on what

> *Your goals are your lighthouse in the crazy storms of life.*

you should do about the other situations in life that are currently causing you unbelievable amounts of stress and headache.

If you give up on your goals in order to focus on the stressor, you only invite more stress by working with a dark cloud hanging over you, the disappointment of not consistently working toward your dream.

PERSPECTIVES CHANGE WITH AGE, BE PATIENT

It's easy to think about what you could've done. When you start looking at how old you are or all the different opportunities you've had and you feel a slight dissatisfaction with what you have accomplished with your time, it's tempting to look back and regret not making certain choices.

This is a poor use of your mind. First of all, if you were to go back in time and have the opportunities you had then, the choices would be the same because you still wouldn't have the knowledge you have now. It would be the same nature-nurture influenced decisions without the possibility of knowing the regret that could come later.

Second, you needed to take the paths you took in order to bring you to the now, the here and now where you still have myriad choices and opportunities for growth and development. Your life is your own story and there is no way of changing the past—you can only live now.

YOU'RE NOT THE SAME PERSON

You are not the same person you were five years ago. There's danger in comparing your life to what might have been or to another who made different choices or someone's life you find more attractive than your own. Comparisons such as these are more fantasy than facts. Embrace your past and be thankful for it—even the things you wish you could've changed have helped to give you all of the positive characteristics you now possess and the opportunities that are before you.

For example, I lacked ambition for many years. I wasn't lazy. By ambition, I mean the desire to achieve some large goal or anything really outside of working and earning money for my daily existence. I thought something must be wrong with me. All of the people who were described as successful—the role models, the folks I was told to look up to in high school—had big goals to be significant and accomplish wonderful things in life. I couldn't think of a single realistic career or goal that I would hold up as my desire.

But as I look back now, instead of regretting the potentially wasted years, I am glad for my lack of ambition.

I have grown into a life filled with goals, challenges, and ideas that I want to give form to; but in early adulthood, my lack of ambition made me a better father to my young children. It allowed me to take more time playing and talking with them when they were young. I wasn't stressed out about some big meeting at the office or some big sale I needed to close. I left my work at work because I knew it wasn't my career, and I would come home mentally free, which allowed me to be present while at home. I believe my aimless perspective during that time helped me establish a solid parent-child relationship that has carried through the years.

It's not always a negative thing to be unsure of what you want to do with the rest of your life, or to have rather vague and not-so-lofty goals for the future. Just let yourself evolve as you may. The world's standards for achievement are not your own. Try to see the positive aspects of the characteristics that make you who you are.

DEALING WITH WAITING

How do you adjust your perspective when you are impatient about something? When you are waiting for an answer to a question, for a package to arrive in the mail, or maybe even a traffic light to change to green when you are late for an appointment, impatience, restlessness, and eagerness can be some of the most the difficult of emotions or feelings to control, but it can be done.

First, see if there is anything that you can do to expedite the process or to get the answer in a proactive way. If there is nothing that can be done at the moment—for example, the traffic light—you must sink into the idea of trusting the process and believing that all will be okay.

Remember, it often comes down to beliefs. In your impatience, you are believing that all will *not* be okay. Let go of that belief and adopt the positive one. This takes practice, but is well worth the effort. When you can calm your impatient mind, you will think more clearly and you may come up with an idea that you may not have thought about while obsessing about the answer, the package, how late you are going to be, etc.

If possible, find a task or a project to work on. When you channel your impatient energy into something else— something useful—you can get ahead in another area of your work and this will help to ease the sense of restlessness in your current mind state.

Choosing to be patient when you are eager or frustrated is a priceless skill that will serve you well throughout life.

YOU ARE AT THE BEGINNING

Whatever it is you want to accomplish, whatever it is you want to create, consider yourself to be always at the beginning. This perspective invites patience. It cultivates a love for the process of becoming, or building. Knowing that you are at the beginning helps to weed out false hopes and expectations and prepare you for the long and short run of life.

Is your goal simply to learn how to change your perspective? You are at the beginning. The learning is the process that gives birth to the change. It might feel like it's sudden when you *realize* that the trajectory of your life has changed, but it is that gradual difference in the way you approach daily life that has been the catalyst. And when you start at the beginning, you will always have more excitement and experiences and growth to look forward to.

PERSONAL REFLECTIONS

- Imagine you are in a jail cell alone for 23 hours a day. As time passes minute after minute, hour after hour, day after day, month after month, and maybe even year after year, what would you do to pass the time? How might this situation affect your perspective of time?

- In what way can you use patience to accomplish your goals?

- Do you compare your pace of living and achieving goals to others'? If so, why?

- What are some ways you can practice focusing on only the current moment rather than looking ahead or behind?

CHAPTER SIX

CREATIVITY

*Thus the materials for the creative product
lie all about us, equally accessible to everyone.
What keeps us from being more creative is a frame
of mind...that persists in seeing only the commonplace
in the familiar. We become frozen in the ice of our
own conservatism, and the world congeals about us.*
—Earl Nightingale

The source for creativity and productivity lies neatly within the mundane. Your daily habits have within them seeds of ideas for stories, projects, and potential sales pitches. The frame of mind that Earl Nightingale references in the above quote is, of course, a person's perspective.

How do you use the power of perspective in order to be more creative?

First, it's not about being more creative. You are already as creative as you need to be. It's about observing and taking action on the creative seeds that are all around you. It's about seeing the boring through the lens of the interesting. For example, if you like movies and work in video production or editing, you might see a story in the images you see every day on your way to work or school.

The way to gain this perspective is to start letting go of the habit of thinking inwardly too much of the time. Too much introspection in daily activities is what often inhibits us from seeing the gold. We are walking or driving to work, but we are thinking about what we need to get done—before we even get to work, we are putting our minds to work. We think about our to-do list and the phone calls we need to make, and maybe even what groceries we will pick up and what bills need paid.

If you want to try something different to stimulate creativity, look around you on your way to wherever you are going. Whether you are going to work or the grocery store or wherever, let your mind take in the pictures like a video camera. This is how most of us think—in pictures. Try not to let the random thoughts turn into a train of thought that gets you lost in your mind in the details of one topic. Instead, imagine you are recording life as it is.

There is nothing to improve on or change or pay special attention to; you are just a spectator. As the film of life rolls by, with the camera in your head you will begin to notice interesting patterns. Recurring images form a theme. A building you've passed a thousand times gives you a fresh idea for your presentation at work. The tree line, a squirrel, a billboard with a loud slogan plastered across it makes you think of a way to improve the home-based business you are working on.

These are not secrets or mysteries; they are only the result of changing your perspective to see what is already all around you as part of the miracle of life.

TAKE A WALK OUTSIDE

There is a reason why people feel more peaceful when enjoying "nature." Nature in this context meaning walking in the woods, lounging at the beach, strolling through a grassy field—being outside. We are part of the natural world. Humans have gained the cognitive abilities to outwit our predators and build safe habitats. Beyond safety, we've built societies based on trust and restraint and mutual respect and all the aspects of what we call civilization. Through this relative safety, we've accumulated and provided more food and clothing than we need in many cases. This progress led to more innovation even to the point where now we can share an idea, a picture, some words of wisdom with people on the other side of the earth by pushing a button or two on our phone.

But we started out as nature.

When the buildings—offices, homes, museums, and hospitals, which of course are wonderful benefits of our progress—become more like prisons to us, it's time to go outside. If you spend eight or ten hours a day staring at a computer screen, taking and making phone calls, composing emails and reviewing documents and files or numbers, it is essential to take a break and get outside. This simple act has a way of defusing or making less serious the events or situations that may be present in our current state of mind. Taking a walk is the best medicine to relieve stress and aid in decision making that many of us need in this increasingly fast-paced society.

CREATE AND SHARE THROUGH SOCIAL MEDIA

The ability to create content and share a message with people worldwide, instantly, is incredible. It's amazing to think that by pushing a few buttons on that small device that we carry in our pocket that we can connect with people globally. You can use social media to make connections you could not form otherwise.

You don't use this forum to form opinions about yourself. Use it potentially to get feedback on your work, to spread awareness about your work, to spread optimism and positivity to anyone who happens to consume your content or your products. But be careful. Don't allow social media to control your life. Don't allow it to distract you from your ultimate desire, your ultimate goal. Instead, use this far-reaching means of communication as a tool to help others become aware of what you have to offer that may improve their lives or lighten their load in some way.

DREAMS AND THE MUNDANE ROUTINE

There are answers to life's problems to be found in your dreams. If you can remember a dream the next day, it's a good idea to write down what you remember. Sometimes, it doesn't even take that much effort. You may remember it clearly and know what you need to do or how to respond to an issue based on the story in your dream.

Our thoughts form stories and they make up our dreams at night too. Just like our thoughts in daily life, sometimes dreams don't make any sense. That's why we can't always trust our thoughts or dreams. They are random and nonsensical. Edgar Allan Poe wrote in a poem that "All that we see or seem is but a dream within a dream."

So how do dreams affect your perspective? Think about the times you had nightmares and you woke up feeling scared. There was be a sense of relief, finally, when you realize it was all a dream and now you are awake in a familiar room—but it took a few minutes to awaken fully, right? There were a few moments when you felt uneasy at best and terrified at worst. Use these dreams to feel gratitude, to understand that life can be scary but that it is okay in the end.

Other times you may wake up from a good dream disappointed to be back in your regular life. Use those type of dreams as motivation to achieve what you once thought was impossible. Use those dreams to imagine the impossible and go after it in real life.

THIRD PERSON PERSPECTIVE

Here is a great hack for using perspective in a creative way to achieve your dreams and goals. Start by writing down your goals in detail, but write them in the third person. Think of everything about the imagined or fantasized situation and goal, every small detail you can think of—write them down. Then write down the part about how you will achieve it, what you will do and say and create, the people you will meet, the collaborations, the networking, the good and the bad—write it all down.

An example of writing in third person: He wanted to be a pastry chef. He saw himself in a kitchen with every utensil needed to create the most delicious and unique pastries the world would ever know. There on the shiny counter was a chocolate tempering machine, pastry comb set, puff pastry rolling pin, whisk, fluted tart baking pan, and measuring spoons and cups. He was amazed because he realized these were all the tools he needed to make his dream come true.

When you are done, read it often, and you will find inspiration to do whatever it takes to make it true. Act it out.

You can also film yourself and make videos of yourself talking about your goals and how you are going to go about accomplishing them. This is a way of releasing your goals as merely thoughts from your mind. Eventually, you can detach yourself from your thoughts about it, and it makes it easier to see things objectively.

Create your story objectively.

You essentially create a story—your story, but it hasn't happened yet. But when you put it on paper or film and then you consume it as a reader or a watcher, it begins to seem as if it is a story outside of yourself like any other book or film you would read or see. However, this one is yours and you can act it out in real life and the things you imagined in your story can come true in real life.

Try this and see if it works for you. It is a change in perspective through the simple act of documenting your story and viewing it as a consumer rather than the creator. Then become the creator by being the protagonist. Eventually begin doing the things you've written about. Make yourself the hero of your story.

PERFECTIONISM

If you must achieve perfection in every undertaking, you won't get much done. Nothing is perfect, which means potentially that everything is perfect. I like to switch perspective on this by imagining that something that is done, complete, and finished is perfect. That doesn't mean one won't find fault with it, but it is perfect when it is finished. It is done. It is time to move on to the next piece of work, the next endeavor, and the next adventure.

You can still take your time and get it as right as possible, but don't let yourself cross that line into thinking that it can be without error, that it will be without critical response or flaw. It's a fine line, but it is noticeable when you have crossed it and come back and finish and call it done when you are tempted to analyze an action or project to the point of uselessness.

Change your perspective about perfectionism by redefining perfect.

THE CREATIVE POWER OF PROBLEMS

Problems force us to use our creativity in ways that are often overlooked during the banality of our typical day.

When problems occur, you might get upset and not see it clearly. So how do you adjust your perspective so that you can see and use the power of problems to your benefit?

1. *Call problems opportunities for solutions.* When you tweak that choice in words, you begin to subconsciously start looking for solutions a bit more quickly following the occurrence of a problem. This change in perspective triggers the creative energy needed to find the solution to the problem and also makes the idea of problems more appealing as you feel the rewards of finding the answers that solve the problems. Opportunities are attractive—problems are not.

2. *Recognize the strength gained from getting through difficult situations.* Think about a world in which you never had any problems. While it might sound lovely at first, upon examination you will see a place that never grows, a world in which nothing is ever challenged— as a result, everything remains the same. People would be as static as the situation they found themselves in. No problems equal no growth, no strength.

3. *Use problems to add to your skillset and confidence.* The trick is to observe your feelings after getting through a problem that you considered to be particularly difficult. Compare your feelings of being overwhelmed or nervous when faced with a problem,

to the calmness, relief, and sense of well-being after solving a problem. Exercise a bit of introspection and see exactly what you learned from the situation and how the next time you face a similar problem, you will be better equipped to handle it. This way of thinking will add to your confidence.

NOTHING NEW UNDER THE SUN

Don't hesitate to do something just because you know it's been done before. It is easy to think that whatever we endeavor to do must be original or must have some sort of unique twist to it in order to be of quality or value. This idea is another example of self-doubt that cripples so many into procrastination and never finishing their objective.

To adjust your perspective about originality, consider that nothing that is produced or done is really original. It is all built upon someone else's work, knowledge, thoughts, and creativity. Most of what we believe is built on our parent's beliefs, authors' writings, movies we've watched, and the people we've encountered who have had an impact on our worldview. Many of our interests were cultivated through childhood experiences. These aspects are what form our outlook.

What is unique about what we do is that it comes from our own minds at a certain time and place. It may not be original, but it is unique in that no one else alive shares our exact DNA code, and that means there are nuances in the way we communicate, in the way we do a thing. What this also means is that there is a way in which we create, work, or produce something that will connect with other similar personalities in a way that other, perhaps more famous, people would not be able to do, even if we are doing the same thing.

Do what comes naturally to you, that is the most important part. Begin whatever it is without worry of people's criticism, most importantly your own criticism which is often the most harsh. The more you do what you are designed to do, the more your own unique twist will become evident.

GAIN INSIGHT FROM DISAGREEMENT

If you allow your emotions to get in the way of what you process mentally, you miss out on opportunities to learn from other people. One of the ways this lesson manifests itself is when two people argue. It doesn't need to be verbal; it could be a business disagreement or some other more indirect form of disagreement; regardless, there is almost always something to be learned from disagreements.

When you dive into another person's world and see the situation from their perspective—and this takes intentional concentration and sometimes discussion with an outside party—you can see variables to the disagreement that you had not noticed or considered before. Understanding a few of the elements that could have caused others to disagree with you, allows you to negotiate with them or concede as necessary. Even if the situation is no longer active, you can understand another piece of human psychology when you analyze and realize the motives and viewpoints of the other person. This knowledge may help you in the future with a similar situation. Be ready to learn from disagreements if you want to strengthen your ability to interact with others.

CREATIVE LISTENING

The skill of listening is a difficult one to attain and use with consistency. Work on listening with a completely relaxed mind. It will take many failed efforts and much practice to get to the point where you can really engage in a conversation and take away all kinds of insight due to your ability to shut out your own mind while listening to the thoughts and ideas coming from another mind.

It won't be an entirely passive ordeal or you would retain nothing, but focus on a couple key areas where we cheat ourselves out of new experiences and ideas from conversations. Release the inclination to formulate your answers, rebuttals, next questions, or verbal responses of any kind until the speaker is completely done talking and it is an opportune time to respond.

Resist the urge to formulate your responses until AFTER the person stops talking.

The mind's ability to come up with words will be enhanced by the improved understanding and interpretation of what was said. The improvement comes from a relaxed mental approach to the conversation. For example, letting go of the pressure to respond in a certain way (whether with humor, intelligence, a certain answer, etc.) allows for more accurate processing of what was heard, and consequently, a more clear and authentic response that may allow the conversation to continue in a meaningful way or may bring it to an abrupt end.

Either way, you'll be more likely to gain information, inspiration, humor, or meaningful conversation for connection's sake if you practice clear-minded listening techniques.

SAVE OR SPEND?

For a more secure financial foundation, get into the habit of saving more than you spend. It is trained into us through the free enterprise system to enjoy and look forward to spending more than saving, but you can influence your psychology to become more balanced in regard to financial expenditures. When you start finding pleasure in seeing the money in your bank account grow, you will be more motivated to save and more reluctant to spend.

It sounds simple, and it is difficult at first, but like everything else, it requires patience and persistence to start seeing that shift in your perspective. Look for balance here as well. You don't want to become so focused on saving that you don't buy things that you or your family need.

Also, it takes a balanced perspective about money to understand that there is a time to spend it and have a good time with your family and friends. If you are saving money all your life to be rich when you retire while sacrificing the good times you could be having now, you might be missing out on some amazing experiences. Understand yourself and your goals, and pay attention to where you might be out of balance when it comes to personal finances.

KEEP YOUR MIND OPEN

Keeping your mind open to new ideas while you work is different from intentionally thinking about a project outside of the one you are working on and should be focusing on. This open-mind perspective is simply to remind yourself that you are not in control of many of the thoughts that arise in your mind; and even when you are working on a project, it is possible and even likely that a thought or an idea about something totally different may come into your mind for a fleeting second before you return your mind to the work at hand.

Pay attention to spontaneous ideas—grab your notebook or phone and write the idea down so you can revisit and explore it deeper when you are able. The main point is to catch those thoughts before they disappear potentially never to return. You have to be careful not to wreck your concentration on the work you are already doing, however. Write down the thought or idea that came to mind and quickly refocus to your current activity.

PERSONAL REFLECTIONS

- Do you consider yourself to be creative? Why or why not?

- In what circumstances do you have your most creative ideas?

- Look around you right now and observe your surroundings without thinking. What stands out to you?

- Do you write your ideas down as quickly as you can?

- Is there someone in your life who will argue with you to make you see other sides of an idea or issue?

- Do you practice the skill of listening to others?

- What creative idea have you come up with from a chance encounter or typical conversation with another person?

CHAPTER SEVEN

EMPATHY AND GRATITUDE

We are all just walking each other home.—Ram Dass

Humans are naturally judgmental. One reason is because being judgmental allows us to avoid dangerous individuals. Especially in primitive times, the quick and accurate judgment of others' motives was an essential skill to have in order to survive. Many times we judge others because we see them as "others" rather than people like us but with different perspectives based on their background.

Everyone has a unique background based on their geographic location of birth, their family circumstances, the way they were raised and the resulting experiences. If you can understand how all this shapes people's view of the world, you can interact with them from a place of empathy rather than otherness.

When you allow yourself to be insulted or offended by an individual whose personality is so different from yours that it is hard to get along, you may be missing an important link in your relationship connections that you need. The offender could be a colleague, a family member, or even a friend. Try a perspective of complete empathy toward those you don't immediately take a liking to. Understand you may have the same attitude and act the same way if you came from where they came from. Don't be so sure that you don't cause the same feelings within them toward you that you have toward them.

Interact with people from a place of empathy rather than otherness.

When you adapt this perspective of empathy, it makes it easier to work with and live with people you don't always enjoy being around. It takes negativity out of the situation because you aren't rushing to judgment and thinking of the negative aspects of someone. Instead, you are open and empathetic. Ask a few more questions of them instead of hurrying to get away, and you will begin to know them as people rather than irritants. In learning more, you will probably be surprised to find a commonality—and maybe another and another.... Really, this should come as no surprise as it was pointed out many years ago that *what we find offensive in others is also found in ourselves.* It may not take the exact same form, but it is within us. Otherwise, we would not recognize it.

As you interact with others, their whole world is within their own minds. The things you think about them are not necessarily true.

> *Everyone is dealing with something you know nothing about.*

What you think they are thinking could be completely wrong. And, don't expect others to see you as you do and don't expect others to think as you would imagine they think.

Everyone lives in their own world. They have grown up differently than you and with different DNA. Their interests and way of seeing the world is their own, just as yours is your own. It is important to be aware of these differences and understand this truth because it allows you to observe others from a more objective perspective. This way you can learn about them and from them. If you bring assumptions to every table of conversation, you judge without knowing, limit their and your interaction, and miss the chance to learn from or help them.

Always remember the saying that everyone you meet is going through something you know nothing about, so be kind. This is a perspective that can improve our lives as individuals but also the lives of humanity collectively.

DON'T JUDGE OTHERS AND DON'T JUDGE YOURSELF

Choose your perspective when you are feeling resentful about someone's behavior or something that was said about you. Let go of judgment by realizing that most criticism is self-judgment. When you resent things about others, it reflects a lack of your own self-assurance. Work on letting go of the offenses of others by:

1. Determining to put only positive energy into the universe—workplace, community, home—through your words, thoughts, and actions.

2. Giving yourself grace when you make mistakes on your journey through life.

3. Focusing on your goals above all other stress and emotion.

By following these three steps, you can quickly erase the judgment you feel about others and yourself. The next time you catch yourself complaining about someone else or feeling unhappy with yourself, remember to drop judgment like a load of bricks. Carrying it with you will only slow you down.

DEVIL'S ADVOCATE

When interested in changing your perspective, consult a trusted partner, friend, or mentor to help you see situations a different way. This may be someone you typically argue with. Arguing can be healthy and extremely useful in changing your perspective. You don't want to vent to someone who is simply going to agree with you and make you feel validated and justified in your complaints and negative opinions.

Be thankful for a friend who can thoughtfully help you see the other side of an issue.

As humans, our inclination is to seek out sympathizers because it satisfies our need for acceptance, but of course this will not expand our minds or alter our perspectives. Find someone who sees things another way. Sometimes this perspective will come from an unlikely source, someone you may not talk with often.

Don't be afraid to ask. Don't be afraid of open dialog and discussion with other minds. We often accept and live by a social stigma that says if you ask for help or advice or if you need to vent about your day, that means you don't have it together, that you aren't a professional at what you do. This is nonsense.

When the mind becomes overactive and begins to convince you of things that are detrimental to your existence, to your daily activities, thought processes, or actions, many times all it takes is to talk to someone else about the negativity you are feeling, and they may be able to cut through the lies and mental trickery because they are not feeling the weight of the emotions that come with the thoughts.

THE LITTLE THINGS

One way we can begin to cut through the negativity is by looking at the little things we take for granted, like being able to feed ourselves, walk, and put our clothes on unassisted, any of these daily activities that we fail to take note of typically speaking. When you stop and find within yourself a little gratitude for the nice day you are having, for the food that you are eating, or for the health you are enjoying as you take a walk or exercise, mentally and even verbally acknowledge these moments. They are gifts, miracles to be experienced with awe.

When you can say *thank you* for the pleasant experiences you have as a human every single day, you will see an interesting phenomenon start to reveal itself to you. Colors will become brighter, your mind will become clearer, sharper in some unmistakable way. Sensations become more powerful. Hearing music, tasting food, watching movies, reading, writing, and talking with a friend—all of these activities take on a feeling of being the first time you are experiencing them. Like going back to your childhood and appreciating once again what you haven't appreciated since then.

Gratitude for pleasant experiences is a little like seeing things through rose-colored glasses, but not the same. It's more natural; it's a perspective that is inside of us all along—that you can choose at any given time to appreciate something about your circumstances. It's one of the most important tools you have for learning how to harness the power of perspective to change your life for the better.

The habit is cultivated by cherishing already existing moments that occur within your daily experience but are buried by worry, stress, or goals that overshadow the beauty of life's simple pleasures.

PRACTICALITY

You may say, "Well, that's not too practical for me. I have places to be and people to see—I don't have time to be sitting around smelling the roses and being thankful that I can smell." But it *is* practical, even necessary to take your time and look at little details with gratitude. Not that it needs to slow you down in noticeable ways—it's more about cultivating and maintaining a state of appreciation for all that enables you to have places to be and people to see.

You can live your life in this state of mind daily, and it is practical to do so because it sharpens your mind and reduces stress. It lightens your mood and allows you to carry less emotion throughout your workday and home life. In turn, these benefits help to improve relationships and goal achievement.

It's always practical to have the skill of controlling your perspective. Even if you go back to your original perspective when dealing with a problem or an obstacle, it is helpful to be able to see a situation from all sides. Maintaining an appreciative mindset enables a clearer picture of all sides.

THE COLLECTIVE CONSCIOUSNESS

Another way to make the best use of perspective in order to achieve your version of success but also gain additional skills in controlling your thinking is to imagine that what you do effects of all humanity. Imagine that the choices you make are with the good of every human being everywhere in mind.

Are they?

Are you conscious of how today's actions could be impacting the collective of humanity? To begin to eliminate your ego as the source of motivation, consider yourself to be the same as others—interested in similar values, life goals, and comforts. If everyone started living from this perspective, we would see the end of war and the beginning of a more peaceful human experience.

We so closely identify with beliefs and differences and nations and politics and borders that we begin to consider others as so different from us that we miss the fact that we are the same. All humans are of one race, the human race. We are different from animals in the ways that we are the same as people. But because we create ideologies and important laws to maintain civility, we end up repressing what is in us that allows us to recognize our similarities. Our humanness. The similarities that want for food, shelter, comfort, and companionship in this experience we call life.

Many times we are too focused on the outside to pay attention to the ever-present connection inside all of us who are alive. In our daily life, it is a valuable perspective to remember in our goals and actions that we are individuals of a whole.

THE ALLURE OF MORE

You may have experienced what it is like to not have enough, and so consider more to be a good thing even to the point of excess. But it is worth considering your perspective on the idea and aspiration of more. When you are offered opportunities in your career to earn more money, consider whether you really need more money. And if you do, why do you need more?

The same with technology, do you need the latest phone or tablet or laptop? And if so, why? Sometimes just because you *can* have more may not be enough reason to have more. It may end up causing you stress or heartache later on. It's a perspective to own when you are presented with opportunities for more. People often don't realize what a source of stress our instinctual desire to have more can be.

Being patient and examining your desire for more is resistance to consumer culture and is useful in that it allows you to focus on the work over the reward. Resisting the urge to chase opportunities for more money or more comforts gives you the focus you need to complete long-term goals and projects. It gives you that coveted gift of concentration.

> *Success comes to those who master their attention, desires, and habits.*

Success comes to those who master their attention, desires, and habits in the way that enables concentration to take over. From this place, history is created. Maintain a perspective that is critical and skeptical about the allure of more.

CONTRADICTIONS OF LIFE

It doesn't always make sense. It won't always make sense. There are moments in life when the thing that you see, the ideal that you held, the life you think you are experiencing turns out to be false. Maybe a commitment is broken without warning, or a loved one is lost in a tragic, unexpected way. *Balancing ideas within your mind and understanding the cyclical nature of existence can help you to be more open* to startling, strange, and sometimes sad occurrences in life.

When you have an balanced perspective, you will see the opportunity to learn and grow from the experience. You will see the chance to help others and consequently make the world a better place. The contradictions and paradoxes are all around us and the more you are able to accept them, the brighter and lighter this life becomes.

ADAPTING TO CHANGE

Change is a disruption of our unconscious programming. This is disturbing to us because it knocks us out of our comfortable existence where we don't have to face the unknown.

Even if you are in a job you don't like, an unfulfilling relationship, and living in the town you always wished you could leave, people have a tendency to remain in those circumstances because change to any routine is almost always unwelcome.

This is an example of the cycle of emotions and thoughts that cause us to do the same things—for the most part—day after day, week after week, and year after year. The thought causes an emotion which causes familiar thoughts and actions that maintain the program.

See change as an opportunity to get out of an endless circle of stagnant existence. At first, it will be uncomfortable, but then, once you accept and embrace the change, it will become exciting—a challenge and a chance to experience new thoughts and emotions.

This skill of adapting to change through controlling your perspective is strengthened—paradoxically—by learning the practice of letting go of control. This topic was discussed thoroughly in Chapter 2 but it is a recurring theme throughout the book. It is mentioned again in this chapter because of the importance of knowing when control is critical—and when it is best to ease up on the reins a bit.

> *There's a crack in everything, that's how the light gets in.*
> *—Leonard Cohen*

SOMETIMES, LET GO OF THE REINS

One reason you might love your routine, no matter how unhealthy, is to have a consistent pattern of thoughts, emotions, and behavior that gives the illusion you have control over your life. Consistency offers the false feeling of safety and permanence. You know well that life does not offer permanence and so, of course, you are not truly safe at all times nor do you ever have full control.

While at face value, this might sound like a terribly negative and depressing outlook, it can be used to your advantage in three ways:

1. Knowing you are not in complete control, you can embrace change and release self-imposed stress and responsibility for safety and security at all times. It's an impossible task to maintain constant stability throughout life. Determine to learn something from each unexpected change in your life.

2. Release the need to be right. Allowing yourself to be wrong—especially about presupposed ideas regarding experiences and other people and minds—can be among the most enlightening choices you make.

3. Stop judging yourself. Letting go of the need to live up to a made-up standard of identity and accomplishment will give you the freedom to actually accomplish more by lightening the load of stress and guilt you carry.

Success in life is heavily dependent on your ability to hold contradictory ideas in your head and see and accept them as they are.

PERSISTENCE PERSPECTIVE

Adopt a perspective of persistence. Do you get frustrated when things don't work out as you hoped or imagined? Of course you do. We all do. But the key to gaining control over the situations in which you become most frustrated is to have a well-established perspective of persistence.

When we have the perspective that no matter how upset we get or how much we want to quit, we will not, then we maintain a defense against the pessimism that grows from repeated failure. The attitude that makes us come back one more time is the key to finally breaking through the thing that is frustrating us.

LAUGH AND LIGHTEN UP

A good laugh can change your perspective on any situation you're facing at any given moment. Try watching your favorite comedy show on TV the next time you are feeling down. If you are stressed out about a big decision you need to make at work, try going to see a standup comedian at the comedy club or searching the Internet for a joke site. Friends who can always make you laugh are invaluable to lightening your mood when surrounded by heavy energy. Laughter helps you see things in a different way.

Laughing has an effect on the mind as well as your whole body by lessening stress and muscle tightness. There is a reason why they say laughter is the best medicine. Surround yourself with people of good humor and who like to laugh as much as you can. There is no need to take the world and life so seriously every minute of the day—we often lose sight of this truth in the worries of our day-to-day existence.

Comedians themselves often find their material simply from taking a different perspective on the daily activities of their fellow humans. Take their cue and appreciate the funny stuff in life. It's all around you!

And don't forget to laugh at yourself at times when appropriate. When you make a mistake or faux pas, rather than getting embarrassed and pretending it didn't happen, own the moment and give yourself—and whoever witnessed the "event"—a great big smile and add a belly laugh. In no time, you will feel better and everyone else will too.

PRESS RESET!

When you are overwhelmed with things to do or there are so many things going on in your mind at once that you feel you nothing is being accomplished, it's time to reset the perspective. Your thinking has to be slowed down periodically or you won't be organized enough to know what to do next. Take a few minutes to reset your mind by:

1. Pausing and breathing deeply.

2. Thinking of something to be thankful for.

3. Making a short list of the top three things to get done and work from that list rather than your long list. It can be three things that you know you can complete in an hour, or it might take you the rest of the day.

The goal is to slow down your mind enough to gain a grateful and optimistic perspective to continue with your work and the activities of the day.

TAKE A BREAK

Taking a break is a great way to reset a negative or pessimistic perspective and come back to work with a renewed zeal, with a positive and optimistic perspective. Take a few days or a week or more, whatever fits your situation, and if possible go away from your home and daily work. Make it a time to relax and laugh and forget about your typical responsibilities and life for a while. It could be alone time or visiting with family or friends or both.

A break from the routine can lead to insights and ideas that will change your life. If you remain open to the possibility, there is no limit to the benefits of seeking a change of scenery and then returning refreshed and renewed and ready to make the most of each day. The wonderful thing is the personal nature of what works to help you see this. Your get-away may mean activity more than relaxation, or a gym rather than the beach, but the main point is to make a break in your routine that allows for a breakthrough in your perspective.

Sometimes all you need is enough time to rest your body and your mind for a while to regain some much needed strength and clarity. But certainly, it is likely that a perspective change can come from a disruption to your daily grind.

STARTING OUT

When you have an idea, a dream, that you are now excited to begin and you are ready to take that first step to making it a reality—that's awesome! Many people have great ideas and wonderful dreams, but they never push themselves to write that first page of the novel or fill out the new-business paperwork, design a website to sell their artwork, or....

If you are reluctant to open yourself up to the world because you are uncomfortable or scared of being seen as a rookie, novice, green, or a wannabe, remember that everyone you see at the top of their game or you consider successful—they all started in the same place and they all had to overcome those same self-doubts and fears you have.

Only a few people are handed success or great wealth and opportunities from their parents or fate—and those people are usually criticized for their luck. It's a no-win situation when you are scared of what others think of you when you are starting out. You just simply have to do it—take the first step.

Don't dread it, rather have fun throughout the adventure and

Celebrate the experience from the beginning.

appreciate the excitement of knowing you are pursuing your dream, your purpose. When you are starting out, you are in many ways as successful as you will ever be— enjoy every moment of being brave enough to try. Many successful people, when asked if they have any regrets about their life journey, say they regret not enjoying more of the moments along the way from the very beginning because they were too focused on reaching the top and achieving their goals.

Keep and maintain a healthy perspective when starting out by remembering that everyone who achieves anything must start somewhere. Celebrate the experience from the beginning.

> *In any given moment we have two options: to step forward into growth or to step back into safety.*
> *—Abraham Maslow*

What does this quote by Maslow mean? It means taking a perspective of meaningful growth and development in every circumstance we find ourselves each day. Meetings, commutes, interactions with strangers, and even morning routines are examples of instances in which we will be faced with this simple choice. Simple in its appearance, but difficult in practice.

Our nature wants to be comfortable because we fear standing out from the crowd, being apart from the tribe. We wish to blend in while, in great contradiction, we feel a pressing need for significance. Not only significance, but achievement. We are capable, but restricted by our fears. Our fear of death and our fear of isolation both motivate us in paradoxical ways; and if we can grasp this truth on a moment-to-

Success in choosing your perspective begins and ends with having empathy for others and gratitude for the opportunities that surround you in life.

moment basis, we can increase the amount of time we spend working toward goals instead of going with the flow.

PERSONAL REFLECTIONS

- What are you thankful for right this moment? Take a minute and write it down.

- Have you practiced empathy for those with whom you have a hard time getting along?

- How can you use empathy when you are criticized?

- When is the last time you had a good laugh? How did you feel afterward?

- How committed are you to step forward rather than step back regarding your goals, dreams, visions, or implementing your ideas?

CONCLUSION

Acknowledge that all you have is this moment right now—you are alive and that is a miracle worth being thankful for. No matter what your circumstances, this outlook is attainable. It is nothing more than a trick of the mind that keeps you down. If you allow your mind to keep you tormented, hateful, bitter, and angry with yourself, you will live a miserable existence. But if you allow your perspective to include empathy for others and joy, laughter, light-heartedness, and love for yourself—you will enjoy a full and exciting life for as long as you live.

Once you believe this, you will experience its power on your mind and your life. Your circumstances will begin to reflect the better perspective of your mind. Essentially, you've taken control of your mind, turning your thoughts about the something negative into something positive. All of life's problems can be lessened by seeing the sunny side, a side that already exists and doesn't need to be made up or imagined, only observed.

Choose your perspective.

USE THE POWER 24/7/365

The beautiful part of gaining control over the power of perspective is realizing that the opportunity to look at your world, the world, your existence in a new and different way is always available—every month, week, day, hour, and minute.

When you find yourself in a funk or state of depression, worry, or annoyance, know that you can always change your perspective. Keep in mind that the mind is malleable—flexible enough to be bent toward the light and away from the dark. Use the power of your positive perspective to get through your every day. But not just get by, but to become and do whatever it is you aspire to do and become. This is the true you. You can use the knowledge presented here and elsewhere to control your outlook on life in any given situation.

This power of perspective is especially useful if you work at a job where you are not content or if you are working every spare moment to start a home-based business. All of the problems you face can be handled and are less important and serious than you imagine them to be. Embrace the power and change your perspective to one that brings you satisfaction and success.

DEFAULT PERSPECTIVES

Your default perspectives should include:

- Positivity

- Gratitude

- Optimism

- Wonder and Awe

- Persistence

- Patience

- Generosity

- Empathy

When you start living from these perspectives, your world will become colored with exciting possibilities. You will find a way to turn the bad news into good news and see brilliant ideas where before was only dust. The sharpness of your mind will increase, the world will be brighter, full of opportunities and places to go and things to do and people to meet. Your *optimistic* attitude will affect you *and* others around you.

Other minds will recognize this freedom in you—the freedom that comes with being able to choose your own outlook on life instead of simply accepting what your mood offers or your life experiences dictate. Because it is all dependent on the mind, when you have a *positive* perspective, you are no longer reliant on external circumstances to be perfect or good for your attitude to be positive. You know now that is now a matter of choice.

Your outlook, attitude, and reactions are each a matter of choice.

Maybe you don't have a carefree outlook each day, but it is okay because you have learned the skills necessary to give yourself the freedom to choose. You can choose to stay focused and exercise your *persistent* perspective and finish that important project ahead of time. And another day you may feel like a distraction is in order, so you choose a more relaxed perspective and see the benefit of taking a break from your work or spending more time with your family. The beauty of controlling your perspective is that it makes everything okay.

Albert Einstein, widely considered an icon of intelligence, said, "It's not that I'm so smart, it's just that I stay with problems longer." *That* is perspective. Patience and effort are the critical components not only in solving problems but also in overcoming the emotional obstacles that often prevent us from being able to choose our perspective.

When we can deploy a perspective of *patience*, it removes the stress that comes from hurrying and not completing "it" quickly enough. When we look at the world through a prism of effort, we understand the law that governs the process of being rewarded for work. Effort and reward are closely related; and when we understand the numerous benefits of quality and consistency when it comes to our endeavors, we will begin to look at life with a perspective that allows us to recognize more opportunities for us to work at the thing God gave us the inclination to work at. We'll begin to do more of what we were made to do.

When there is a shift from focus on reward to focus on effort, the scales will begin to slightly tip and balance out. We will begin to put forth more and more effort,

Look at life with eyes wide open.

contributing to the universe in a meaningful way, helping others; and over time, we will begin to see the rewards of those efforts manifest in our lives.

When we choose to give instead of receive, our perspective as well as our external reality will take on new structure and meaning. For it is what we build that matters, not how much we gain. Our financial wealth is secondary to what our legacy will built for future generations and for humanity as a whole. Maintain hope for a better future and that will inspire the hard but fulfilling work of the present.

A perspective of *wonder*—the world we have built for ourselves, the natural world as well, look at all the comforts and conveniences that most people have today—how can we not be amazed at the wonder of it all? When you can adopt this perspective of *awe* on a daily basis, colors will be brighter, the moment will be more pleasant, and time will slow down. Miracles are all around us. To be alive and experience a full and joyful life is the greatest miracle of all. Unfortunately, we have taken everyday gifts for granted too many times. Work on looking at everything anew, with a fresh perspective like a young child—with eyes wide open. And this is how you grow.

> *In all affairs it's a healthy thing now and then to hang a question mark on the things you have long taken for granted.*
> —Bertrand Russell

Develop the habit of finding a new way of looking at things. From this step of personal growth comes a freedom that cannot be explained, only experienced. It is perhaps the most critical aspect of your personal development journey because it will influence the outcome at every turn. Being grateful for the opportunity and chance to take the journey itself can be the guiding sentiment. *Gratitude* prepares the mind to adjust and embrace the other perspectives as they are called upon.

Generosity and openness, transparency and authenticity, these are the characteristics that allow us to share our personal journey with all who might be helped by it. Never underestimate the power of your story or the power of sharing. When you get to the place where you love yourself and embrace and own up to your past, your story, all the things you used to hide, be ashamed of, and regret about your past, then you are empowered to live without the burden of your past. You own your story; you own your life.

You own your story, within the limits of what you can control of course, but there is one aspect of life that most people cannot get past—their past—the things that used to define them. You can overcome what people say about you and what other people believe about you when you realize you have the power to discard all that. You have the power to realize that what other people think and say simply doesn't matter all that much. *You* get to write whatever story you want to write. If you don't like the first twenty-five chapters (years) of your life, fine, write the remaining chapters the way you see your future—then develop that main character and make him or her into what you want.

All the world's a stage, and all the men and women merely players: they have their exits and their entrances; and one man in his time plays many parts...
—William Shakespeare

Life is a play. It's a game of forming the reality you want to experience and there's no power quite like owning your story.

Once you learn to be flexible with your perspective in every situation, you won't go back to status-quo thinking. You may never be able to abide by that common level of thought again—a welcome change. When you experience the freedom and success that comes through intentional thinking, you will be fascinated by the different levels of your life in which you can use it to improve.

There are so many ways to see everything in life—so many choices of how to perceive an event, a conversation, or some chance encounter. Learn to live with an open mind and an acceptance of life that leads to much more beauty and success in your personal goals. It doesn't matter if people think your perspectives are silly, useless, or unrealistic. Many perspectives could be argued to be useless when it comes down to it; but as time passes, many that seemed to be impractical have proven otherwise.

If you learn to accept yourself for who you are, you will accept others as they are—and that is a wonderful place to be in life—in the world. Acceptance is closely related to empathy in that you can look beyond the superficial aspect of a drama and into how the person is

Accept yourself and you will accept others.

feeling and reacting during a certain situation. Accepting people as they are, and yourself, eases the stress of holding and being held to standards too high to reach.

When we can reach out and help others to be the best and see the best in themselves, when we can help others recognize and achieve goals in life, when we know we have done the right thing regarding how we treat others and ourselves—then we can say with great confidence that we have chosen the perfect perspective.

Remember, freedom begins in the mind—and with intentional thinking, you are free to choose your perspective!

Thank you for reading! If you enjoyed this book, please leave a brief review on your online bookseller of choice.

ABOUT THE AUTHOR

JOHN MARTIN has authored two other books titled: *Empower Yourself* and *Increase Your Personal Productivity*. His content provides tools and steps to analyze your mindset and strip away the beliefs you hold that are untrue and limiting your potential, and also help you to take action regardless of your current situation.

In addition to writing, John enjoys hanging out with his family, reading, cooking, watching movies, and riding along for whatever adventure is next.

ACKNOWLEDGMENTS

Thank you to Dave Wildasin, Nate Martin, Susan Ramundo, Eileen Rockwell, Angela Shears, and Lisa Ott for helping to make this book.